CW00621468

Reinhard Heydrich: The Ideal National Socialist

Translated from Three Original SS Publications

Reinhard Heydrich: EinLeben der Tat
Die Wandlungen unseres Kampfes
Reinhard Heydrich

Plus a Biography written postwar

Table of Contents

Publisher's Introduction

Reinhard Heydrich: The Ideal National Socialist is translated from THREE original SS publications.

The first publication, *Reinhard Heydrich: Ein Leben der Tat* (literally "A Life of the Deed"), was commissioned by the German State Minister for Bohemia and Moravia, SS-Obergruppenführer K. H. Frank *as a token of gratitude to the man who, in a serious hour in the most recent history of Bohemia and Moravia, promptly crushed the plot against the Reich from this region with all the means at his disposal, thereby establishing the groundwork for a positive development in all spheres.* The occasion was what would have been Heydrich's fortieth birthday on March 7, 1944. It includes both articles *about* Heydrich AND three speeches *by* Heydrich.

The second publication, *The Changes in Our Struggle*, was written by Heydrich himself.

The third publication, entitled simply *Reinhard Heydrich*, is a compilation of eulogies by Bormann, Daluege, Himmler and Hitler. It also includes some quotes from Heydrich.

Finally, a short sketch of Heydrich's life, written *after* the war, fills in the gaps.

The Publisher
April 2004

When all others are disloyal, we remain loyal...

I.
A Life of the Deed

The solution of all problems is only possible, if one tackles them as an uncompromising National Socialist.

Reinhard Heydrich

Introduction

On March 7, 1944 Reinhard Heydrich would have turned 40. This date - so significant for Bohemia and Moravia, where he was last active - is the reason for this overview of his activity, which within just a few years elevated him to the highest positions in the party and the state. Although he only had eight months as Deputy Reich Protector - in addition to his position as Chief of the Security Police and the Security Service - in which to put his extensive political, cultural and social-economics ideas into action, his ideas nonetheless live on in the men who have taken over his rich legacy. Eight months are just a short span in the life of an individual man. In terms of the development of a folk, they seem to be nothing. But for Bohemia and Moravia they were a period of transformation and a new order, due to the formative personality of Reinhard Heydrich, whose work remains unforgotten. The "heartland of the Reich" saw a new man at his head, who had much to give it and whose radiance with be felt for long to come.

When his mortal remains left the old German Kaiserburg in Prague on gloriously beautiful day of June 7, 1942, they were carried through the whole city in a ceremonious procession, passing the silent monuments of Prague's German history. Everyone for whom history is not merely a coarse of events, but instead sees in them the work of creative men, felt that Reinhard Heydrich's work could not and was not wiped out. Only so can Reinhard Heydrich's martyrdom seem meaningful to us. The publication of this booklet, commissioned by the German State Minister for Bohemia and Moravia, SS-Obergruppenführer K. H. Frank, is hence a token of gratitude to the man who, in a serious hour in the most recent history of Bohemia and Moravia, promptly crushed the plot against the Reich from this region with all the means at his disposal, thereby establishing the groundwork for a positive development in all spheres. At the same time, however, they are a reminder and obligation to the men who have received the difficult but thankful task to work in Bohemia and Moravia in Reinhard Heydrich's spirit, so that this region, which Bismarck once called "Europe's citadel", becomes one of the Reich's strongest pillars and every inhabitant feels secure.

The contents of this publication are intended to convey a broad picture of Reinhard Heydrich's personality and work.

An in-depth treatment of his work as Chief of the Security Police and of the Security Service is contained in Wilhelm Spengler's essay

"Reinhard Heydrich, Work and Essence". His fundamental work shows not only the wide scope of the activity of the Security Police and the Security Service, but also the deep ethnical core of the new tasks Reinhard Heydrich gave the German political police.

SS-Obergruppenführer K. H. Frank's essay, "Reinhard Heydrich's Work for Bohemia and Moravia", a review of Reinhard Heydrich's eight month work as Deputy Reich protector, shows in detailed summary how many pressing issues Reinhard Heydrich tackled and mastered - or he at least prepared for their solution by establishing guidelines - in such a surprisingly short time.

The ideological essay "The Wenzels Tradition" reveals how much Reinhard Heydrich himself dealt with the historical foundations for his task in Bohemia and Moravia, and how he endeavored to show the Czech folk their constructive path into the Reich in light of their own history. His speech on the occasion of the re-opening of old the German cultural center, the Rudolfinums in Prague, where he affirmed music as the mediator of genuine beauty, his words to the maids of the Reich Work Service discrediting the enemy's slogan about the militarization of the German woman, and his veterans memorial speech on March 15, 1942, are all documents of his manhood. Seldom has this found, intellectually and racially, such a noble embodiment.

Walter Wannenmacher's essay "Reinhard Heydrich", written after the Deputy Reich Protector's death, portrays Reinhard Heydrich's statesmanly logic and continuity in the political formation of the region Bohemia-Moravia.

The comprehensive evaluation of Reinhard Heydrich's personality and life work is provided in the eulogy by the Reichsführer-SS on the occasion of the state burial of the fallen SS-Obergruppenführer on June 7, 1942 in Berlin. His words, dedicated to the fallen comrade and fellow fighter, reveal that Reinhard Heydrich, along with Horst Wessel, were National Socialists who were taken from us all too early. They were capable of, and called to, great things.

Chronology

March 7, 1904
Born in Halle on the Saale

1922
Enlistment in the navy

1926
Lieutenant Junior Grade

1928
Lieutenant Senior Grade

1931
Enlistment in the SS

July 29, 1932
SS-Standartenführer and Chief of the Security Service of the Reichsführer-SS

1933 SS-Brigadenführer

June 17, 1936
Chief of the Security Police and the Security Service

1940
Elected President of the International Criminal Police Commission

1941
SS-Obergruppenführer and General of the Police

September 27, 1941
Deputy Reich Protector

May 27, 1942
Assassination attempt in Prague

June 4, 1942
Death in Prague

Life and Work

The SS – the Security Service and the Security Police are part of this SS – is a shock troop of the party in all matters relating to the internal security of the region and to the protection of the National Socialist idea. Shock troop means that it is always ahead of the bulk, that it is especially well-armed and ready for action and knows how to fight. Shock troop also means, however, that it does nothing contrary to the will and planing of the overall leadership. Prerequisite for the task of the protection of the idea is a deep feeling and probing thought into the problems and action based on knowledge of the problems - not just a superficial view, rather an in-depth study of matters. Therefore, it cannot simply be an executive, external view and fulfillment of matters and of orders. We act as an executive organ in the consciousness of the mission of the Führer and of the Reich – that mission which by means of the Greater German Reich leads to a happier future.

Reinhard Heydrich, October 2, 1941

Wilhelm Spengler

Reinhard Heydrich: Work and Essence

A time like ours - full of a rush of world-historical events, as if world history itself is breathing faster - must be more forgettable than others times, because the present demands all our energy and our gaze is fixed at the Reich's future.

But when the anniversary of the Reinhard Heydrich's death as a martyr for the Reich approaches, we can nonetheless say: He is not forgotten! Quite the opposite, our inner eye now sees the basic elements of his work and essence more clearly after this year interval. What is immortal in this work has been stamped more deeply into our consciousness. No one can measure what the Reich lost in him. Like so many of our folk's best sons, their early death

11

meant the deeds of their later, mature manhood remain undone. The people around Reinhard Heydrich could see how much he belonged to those men who grew with each task, and how his life ended in the middle of this constant growth. This never ending growth of his personality, his tireless productivity and drive provide the sad, absolute certainty that his death cost the Reich not just a one-time creator, but also an unborn work. But even a completed accomplishment for the Reich has – in accordance with the nature of his political assignment – remained hidden from the general public to this day. The public could only sense it when the Führer bestowed on the fallen Reinhard Heydrich, as the second German, the highest decoration that any German can receive, the Highest Level of the German Order, and spoke these words in memory of the deceased: "He was one of the strongest defenders of the German Reich idea, one of the greatest opponents of the enemies of this Reich."

His achievement was - for the first time in the Reich, previously fragmented in many provincial and territorial traditions - to develop through years of tireless constructive work a Reich-wide standardized political police, filled with a completely new sense of purpose, and a comprehensible political intelligence service as an instrument that was always ready for action, effective, reliable and professional. The external process: in 1931 the 27 year old radio and communications lieutenant senior grade left the navy and joins a small SS unit in Hamburg as a SS-private in Hamburg's red districts during the time of struggle. Already in July of the same year the Reichsführer-SS calls him to the Munich Reich leadership and gives him a new task there: to create for the movement an effective political intelligence service, capable in every aspect. That was the birth hour of the Security Service, the SD. After the rise to power the Reichsführer-SS assigns him the political division of the Munich Police Presidium, from which he forms within a few weeks the Bavarian Political Police. In fast sequence the political police divisions of all the other provinces except for Prussia are reorganized based on that example. On April 20, 1934 the Secret State Police of Prussia becomes the final brick in this newly emerging formation. In 1936 a Führer decree brings the Reich Police and Heydrich, 32 years old, becomes the chief of the Security Police and the SD, so that the SD, the Secret State Police and the Criminal Police of the Reich all stand under him.

It is important to recognize the inner nature that Heydrich, in accordance with Reichsführer-SS's directives, gave to this part of the young police of the National Socialist Reich, and the basic world-view considerations from which he started. One of the tragic facts of German history is that in the past the German Reich did not possess a comprehensive political intelligence service working in the Reich's interest. This was tragic in terms of foreign and domestic affairs. Tragic in terms of foreign affairs, because foreign intelligence services, developed with a long tradition – the English Intelligence Service, the French Deuxieme Bureau, the Czarist Ochrana and the Soviet GPU – had long examined the world constellations and evaluated them for their countries, before Germany's turn came. Tragic in terms of domestic affairs, because the various government leaders were so ill-informed about the state's weaknesses and the real situation among the people, that even measured intended to produce aid and relief became counterproductive. Let us remember the 1917 Kaiser speech to the armaments workers in the west, when the Kaiser wanted to master the first crises through his own words, but in ignorance of the real situation selected his words so badly that his speech only made things worse.

When the National Socialist leadership had firmly decided to create such a political intelligence service, the question arose how much of the nature and methods of the already existing foreign intelligence services could be adopted for the apparatus to be developed new for Germany. An absolutely decisive fact was that these intelligence services could in no way be copied. Instead, the Reichsführer-SS and Reinhard Heydrich developed their SD and Political Police to have a totally different nature, which corresponded to the basic ideas of the National Socialist worldview and the natural prerequisites of German man. The race idea is the central idea of National Socialism, from which its folk concept is derived. We have the unshakeable faith that the highest biological values of human existence are present in Germanic-German man, but that in the course of its history the German folk has failed to achieve the total self-realization and self-expression of its nature, because alien world-views and power-political limitations again and again got in the way. National Socialism strives for nothing other than, for the first time in its history, to enable for the German folk the self-realization of its nature in new life orders, life forms and sufficient living space. That simultaneously provides the basic positions for a political Reich police and a political intelligence service. If an intelligence service is to emerge as a link between this individually many-colored, rich in tradition, many-branched German folk and its political leadership - which is supposed to inform this leadership of all developments and dangers within the folk body in the most diverse spheres of life, landscapes and strata, in order to again and again give the leadership information to eliminate danger and promote the positive self-portrayal of German man in new life orders - then the bearers of such an intelligence service and such a political police can certainly not be agents and spies, terrorists and other defective characters, rather men who belong to the German folk

13

with all their heart, who know and understand it from the inside out, and who are totally committed to service for and behalf of this folk. In this sense the SS is destined to be the core troop of this political intelligence service and of this police, because it possesses in its men and clans the realization of German manly and human virtues as the highest life obligation. And this same SS became the bearer of the political Reich police, because only its own highest and total commitment to the Reich of the Germans and the faith in its idea and its mission can provide the insight and at the same time the hardness to recognize and combat all anti-Reich and anti-folk forces in every form and disguise. In this sense Reinhard Heydrich viewed the nature, selection, training and schooling of his men as the decisive foundation for a totally new purpose of a political police and of a political intelligence service. From the former jailer work of the police gradually grew a worldview-formed, shaped from the inside state protection corps for the security of the Reich. Reinhard Heydrich and his men did not care if hostile foreign powers poured buckets of defamation on the German "Gestapo" and the SD. They could only measure their own shoes, the Intelligence Service, the GPU etc., because they worldview foundation of this new German police remained hidden and incomprehensible. This was even more so, because the disseminators of such atrocity tales at home and abroad were racially and intellectually-worldview-wise the personalities of anti-Reich forces, who had already come to feel and appreciate the effectiveness and pitilessness of this new Reich instrument.

Heydrich had taught his men to no longer think and work in terms of "individual incidents", but to view and evaluate each action in the great life context of the German folk evolution. The anti-Reich forces had to be caught in their last intellectual and personnel connections. Already in 1935 Heydrich had given his men the motto that two things are decisive for the successful continuation and completion of the struggle for the Reich: "Correct recognition of the opponent in his deepest essence and the uniform view of one's own tasks as well as one's own mistakes with all the prerequisites and consequences." The Reichsführer-SS has confirmed this in his eulogy: "By the beginning of 1938 the Security Police apparatus was already largely firm in every aspect and equipped for all tasks. It can be safely said today that Heydrich played a big role in the bloodless march into Austria, the Sudetenland, Bohemia and Moravia as well as the liberation of Slovakia, because of his careful identification and conscientious comprehension of all opponents as well as a usually very detailed overview of the enemy's activity, organizations and leaders in these countries." Based on this ordering of all individual cases into the entirety of the folk by their significance and danger for the community, Heydrich carried out the inner reformation of the criminal police.

Who would have in the past considered criminal offenses like theft, robbery and murder to be political acts!?! But at the moment when these offenses are not viewed in terms of the civil perpetrator, but as an offense against the ordely life of the community and as a reduction of the constructive folk strength, the criminal act enters the sphere of folk-political significance. Seen from the life of the community, the pursuit and conviction of the already committed crime sinks to a purely secondary action. Primary is the preventive combat of crime, which on the one hand saves the community from viollations and disruptions by criminals, and on the other hand creates the life conditions for criminally inclined people that keep them from going on the prowl. Heydrich's vastly new ways are reflected in the fact that he was elected President of the International Criminal Police Commission in 1940.

The second essential characteristic that Reinhard Heydrich impressed on his Security Police and his SD was the inner dynamics of this apparatus. Just like since the rise to power the Reich's leadership was again and again faced with ever new tasks and problems at a truly revolutionary tempo, so did this state protection corps, although still just in formation, have to be shaped as an instrument of this leadership, mobile, adaptable and capable of development, so that at any moment it could keep pace with these new Reich tasks. Already in 1935 Heydrich gave his men the short instruction publication he had entitled "The Changes of Our Struggle", and whenever the leadership was faced with new tasks and problems, he always transformed these new problems into the assignment of political-police and intelligence service tasks in addresses to his leadership corps. He often demanded total performance from his men with this inner dynamics of his apparatus. He preferred to be considered too hard or lacking understanding when he removed co-workers who seemed inadequate to him instead of endangering the task for the Reich. For example, in the years after the rise to power the SD could limit itself to above all investigating the worldview and political opponent, Freemasons, Jews, Marxists, communists and politicizing clerics in their effects and connections within the folk body. Just a few years later it was much more important to determine which forces, traditions, local developments and conditions opposed the realization of National Socialist goals in the most diverse life spheres of economy, culture, administration etc.. A comprehensible, objective insight into the most diverse occupations and life connections was the first prerequisite for an intelligence service in this regard. Finally, when the war made the war potential of the German folk a priority political factor for the Reich leadership, the political intelligence service had to continually provide the leading offices of the party, state and armed forces with the information necessary to make judgements about the many war measures. The work perspectives of the political police have already changed considerably. A numerically incomprehensively small apparatus must solve numerous tasks. The political-police security task for the old Reich has expanded to the security task for almost all of Europe. Small commandos must perform very important tasks, from northernmost Norway to the southern tip of the Balkans, from the occupied lands in the west to the bandit areas in the vast Russian spaces. The picture of Heydrich's work would be incomplete without remembering that the following entrusted to him was led to a great extent by his personal example. What he demanded from his men in terms of performance, tenacity and endurance, ceaseless self-development, cleanness and simplicity of personal life, Heydrich had not just demanded of himself, but exemplarily achieved. He was a knight-like personality, even in the conflict with the opponent. That he was a splendid fencer and athlete meant more in his case than a sport virtue, for it perceptively encompassed the structure of his nature. The highest personal respect bound his following to him, for each knew how tirelessly he worked, how simple his life style was, how he was unsurpassed in quick comprehension and swiftly made decisions that met the essence of an issue, how processed tasks were inextricably impressed on his memory and how all threads of this widespread apparatus securely led to his decisive hand. He was a real leader to his following, because he was in all ways the first in this community. Certainly, it corresponded to the nature of his office as chief of the political intelligence service and the political Reich police, which are concerned with all areas of life, that a vast fullness of life events and life problems flowed together. For his co-workers it was always surprising how he grasped and processed all these issues with such a range of intellect and direct personal interest, regardless whether they were problems of economics, ethnic politics, education, administration, schools, treatment of minorities, science, art, folk culture, church politics etc.. That is why, a year after his death, when our gaze falls upon his picture in our office, this is more than just remindful looking; it is often like a personal meeting that gives us confidence and strength. Moments emerge from memory that reflect Heydich's nature with special precision. So it is with that advice he gave to his commandos on the march eastward: "Be hard where you must be hard, be kind where you may be kind."

Karl Hermann Frank

Reinhard Heydrich's Work for Bohemia and Moravia

When Reich Protector Freiherr von Neurath fell ill at the end of September 1941, I was summoned to the Führer headquarters to deliver a presentation about the political situation in Bohemia and Moravia. After in-depth discussions, the Führer decided on September 27, 1941 to entrust the leadership of business in Bohemia and Moravia to SS-Obergruppenführer and General of the Police Reinhard Heydrich. Heydrich was called to the Führer headquarters to take over the full power of authority. I there had the opportunity to become better acquainted with the Chief of the Security Police and the SD. In the headquarters, on the trip back to Berlin and in several conferences in his office, he discussed the situation, made decisions about the leadership of the office and formulated plans about the political line and formation of Reich politics in Bohemia and Moravia. Heydrich, his political skill schooled and honed through years of work, enthusiastically went to work and quickly learned his new task and all the work, so that the difficult problems could soon be solved. As unexpected and surprising as Heydrich's selection was for most people, so too did the purpose and task of this appointment seem to be at first sight, and it seemed possible to figure out how his future execution of duties would proceed. The immediate task Heydrich confronted upon his arrival was initially of a purely political nature. He summed it up back then in the precise words: "I must make the Czech populace realize that they can not get past the realities of their belonging and obedience to the Reich." We must remember that at the end of September 1941 the anti-German wave again swelled considerably; the outbreak of hostilities had led to pan-Slavic-Bolshevik rallies. An illegal military and political organization, equipped with the modern means of terror and sabotage, tried to win political influence and leadership among the masses. This resistance movement had more than just short-wave radio transmitter enabled close contact with emigrant circles in London; it had a secret supporter in the Minister-President of the autonomous government who did not shy from betraying his word as an officer and pretending devotion and loyalty to the Reich Protector while at the same time being in league with the attack against the Reich. The front of active and passive resistance led from the highest figure in the autonomous government to the ministers down to smugglers, swindlers, saboteurs and Jews. The methods - with which Heydrich struck and destroyed the most dangerous opponents in a few days and the entire illegal apparatus in a few weeks - already revealed the political instinct with which he ordered measures beyond the necessity of an executive purification. An outside observer would have hardly noticed during those weeks, aside from the curfews, that he was the witness of the crushing of a systematically prepared revolt. Wehrmacht and police units did not march and there were no armed confrontations. Heydrich's blow was also not directed against the mass of fellow travellers, who were merely the product of illegal agitation. He grabbed the heads of the revolt and hence the main culprits without regard for the rank of the state offices they held. The result of the trial of Minister-President Elias, his extensive confession as well as the summary trials of several generals and officers of the former Czechoslovakian army, and the trials of high ministerial officials right down to the little, incorrigible fanatics, proved the precision of the operation. Since the Jew had in the context of this resistance work shown himself to be the germ of all political destruction, this issue was simultaneously taken up; the Jews were identified and put in ghettos.

After just a few weeks not only the immediate task was solved and the serious threat to security eliminated, but beyond that it was possible despite the severity of the measures to gain initially individual, positive, understanding voices among the Czech folk. The reason for this is that Heydrich was never content with the purely negative goal of a security measure, rather he strove to achieve a positive purpose, even if through a necessary, negative measure. The way of combatting economic parasites most clearly demonstrates this. Without doubt a large portion of the Czech rural population, following the example of the leading men of the Czech Ministry of Agriculture, had hidden about a quarter of the grain supply from the statistics. Severe action against identified parasites combined with an understanding leniency in the effort not to make the little guy suffer for the mistakes of his leaders, led to the unpunished late reporting of grain supplies equaling 20% of the previous figures, while the late reporting of swine yielded the figure 560,000. What these numbers mean for food policy becomes clear when one learns that they made the previously necessary importation of grain from the Reich superfluous.

In his speech to the German leadership and administration apparatus on October 2, 1941, Reinhard Heydrich started with these words: "Gentlemen! You generally see in me the Chief of the Security Police and the SD, hence you generally see a man of the executive. This view is misleading and false." These words contain the affirmation of a man who saw his activity not as a purification action, rather in their total character as a task of political construction. Reinhard Heydrich made this true already in the first weeks of his activity in Prague. Even then one could recognize that he was not just a representative of executive intervention and police prevention, rather a man of statesmanly, creative initiative. This attitude also explains the serious efforts for an orderly development of Czech folk life. It must also be understood that Heydrich, as the man compelled to take the probably most serious and severe measures towards the Czech folk, also showed them the constructive and political concept of the Wenzel tradition - that historical teaching that even a thousand years ago showed the Czech folk the road to the Reich as the only life-preserving conception. The ceremony in the Wenzel chapel of the Prague castle on November 19, 1941 - where State President Dr. Hácha gave seven keys to the coronation chamber to the Deputy Reich Protector and received three of them back for loyal hands - symbolically sealed the relationship of trust between Reinhard Heydrich and the State President on the basis of this intellectual foundation. The Deputy Reich Protector repeatedly received the Czech press, because he desired a truthful interpretation of his measures in the media, in order to gain a growing relationship of trust with the the population of Bohemia and Moravia. How far this succeeded is shown by the results of the measures in the social and agrarian-political area. Combatting black-marketeering, he took the position that seized wares should above all go to the benefit of the working populace, because they had been taken from them. Therefore, he supplied factory lunchrooms preferably through distribution of seized foodstuffs. Beyond that he intensely studied the issues of the salary problem, the nutrition and clothing of workers and their care. Already on October 28, 1941 he was able – with the Führer's approval – to order the same fat rations for two million workmen as in the old Reich. By using confiscated monies from black-marketeers, it was possible to place 200,000 pairs of work shoes at the disposal of the Czech workers free of charge. The regulations for improvement of social security insurance on April 1, 1942 as well as the related recreation action for armaments workers in Bad Luhatschowitz are a fine expression of his socialistic thought for the interests of the Czech workers. In the agricultural sphere, his interventions brought fertile results. He convinced the Czech peasant that poor production hurt him most. Because he realized that the coexistence of numerous agricultural organizations, clubs and associations stood in the way of rational agricultural production - because these organizations were not tools of folk nutrition, rather "factors of a political influence" - he created the prerequisites for the emergence of the present unified federation in the sphere of agriculture. Furthermore, it is characteristic that it was Reinhard Heydrich who made the Czech worker and peasant "socially acceptable" in the Prague castle. The first receptions of Czech worker and peasant delegations in the rooms of the Prague castle took place under him. In addition to this special concern for the workers and peasantry, he strove to give the protectorate's economy the rank it deserved in the Reich due to its significance and performance. This found clear expression in the fact that the assembly of the Southeastern European Society took place in Prague on December 17, 1941. In his introductory words at the assembly he clearly outlined the tasks of the protectorate's economy in the context of the overall economy of southeastern Europe, and beyond that he offered Bohemia's and Moravia's cooperation with the economic integration of the newly won land in the east. This shows on the economic level the long-range view from which he presented tasks to the protectorate. Because the political line practiced in the protectorate did not have the effect of short-term measures, rather strove for the creation of a stabile, domestic political foundation in Bohemia and Moravia, the reformation of the Czech autonomous government and the reorganization of the whole administrative apparatus could not be bypassed. In his address of January 20, 1942 to the members of the government – newly formed by the State President with his approval – he did not call the legal-political event a "normal change of people", rather a "historically significant change of direction". The new government should form with him "the circle of leadership and work, based an mutual trust, for the solution of all tasks in this region". Since clear trust also requires clear responsibility, in the new government he abolished the previously practiced principle of collective responsibility of the College of Ministers, which was in reality collective lack of responsibility, and replaced it with the principle of department responsibility of each Minister. The administration reform represented an even greater act of trust, which – like the Youth Service Duty – he presented in its basics at a press conferfence the day before the assassination attempt against him. The main point of the administration reform was the massive reduction of the German administrative apparatus in the protectorate and the transfer of most of its affairs to the autonomous administration. Far from any departmental egoism, in anticipation of the requirements of personnel reduction in the present winter - and in accordance with the idea of Bohemia's and Moravia's autonomous self-leadership – Heydrich reduced the Reich-owned administrative apparatus to the bare minimum.

The introduction of the Youth Service Duty for the Czech youth corresponded to the widely expressed need of open-minded Czech circles worried about the danger of a nihilistic decline of their youth. Since Heydrich himself had grown up under the natural laws of a healthy youth movement, he was especially near to these issues. He recognized that "Bohemia and Moravia can only keep pace with development, if its youth also enjoys an education corresponding to Bohemia's and Moravia's task in the Reich." It must be pointed out that through introduction of the Youth Service Duty Reinhard Heydrich gave Czech youth a European-quality educational opportunity and had performed an act of equal rights compared to the other folks; without the Reich's help, the Czech youth would not have been capable of this. Precisely this initiative for the benefit of the Czech folk was the reason for the criminals in London to give the final order for murder.

A tribute to Reinhard Heydrich's work for Bohemia and Moravia would not be complete, if one did not remember his services to the Germandom of this region. Here, too, he used both hard intervention as well as a positive formation of life. His first executive measures were simultaneously aimed at the war-profiteers who pretended "to work in the Reich's interests, but in reality were here only for the sake of their own profits and hence hurt the Reich's image". He stood with much emphasis against the elements of folkish unreliability and placed the demand on the Germans of this region that they first of all present an example of a spotless National Socialist bearing before any justified or unjustified claims. "Enemy of all enemies and guardian of everything German", in this SS-attitude, he once said, did he see his task for Germandom in Bohemia and Moravia. His preference was for the German culture in this region. The singularly of Prague's architecture deeply impressed him. He was able to interest Reich Minister Speer in Prague and arrange a visit in Prague, which was filled with fruitful architectural plans for the Prague's architectural development after

victory. German institutions of higher learning found a special pro-
moter and protector in Reinhard Heydrich. The oldest Reich university
was to not just preserve a rank appropriate for its tradition, but also be
a pioneer in the permeation of science with the folkish necessities of
the Reich. It is characteristic that the majority of new professor chairs
created under him involved folk-sciences. Beyond that, he created the
prerequisites for a Reich sponsorship of ethnology and arts research,
which after his death received the name "Reinhard-Heydrich-
Foundation".

Again and again, he directed his attention to Prague's German thea-
tres. Above all, thanks to him the budget for the establishment of a
German operetta was approved.

His plans included establishment of an ongoing opera in Prague. On
the occasion of the opening ceremony of the Rudolfinums on October
16, 1941, he proclaimed the bestowment of the Reich Protector's Culture Prize on three German artists. His closest bond, howeever, was
with music. His interest in music corresponded to his artistic gift,
since he came from a well-known family of musicians in Halle. His
special interest was the German Philharmonic Orchestra. He played a
special role in the formation of the Prague Music Weeks in 1942, during whose introduction he said, "Music is the creative language of artistic and musical people as the conveyer of their inner life." The evening before his assassination attempt he attended a house music evening in Waldsteinsaal, where a work by his father was performed by his
own previous coworkers, a quartet from Halle. So just a few days before his death the music-filled world of his parents' house emerged as
allegory, from which Reinhard Heydrich's life as a fighter had started.
Only truly great men manage to, in just a short span of their activity,
manifest an energy that shapes both present and future. From Reinhard
Heydrich sprang this energy that survives death. The diversity of the
tasks given him, the clarity of his political sight, but above all the unprecedented impulse of his leader personality justify us when we
speak of Reinhard Heydrich's political legacy for Bohemia and
Moravia. It was established in that short time span between September
1941 and May 1942 in comradely cooperation, and we have obligated
ourselves to its uncompromising fulfillment in frontof Heydrich's coffin.

Reinhard Heydrich's Speeches

The Wenzels tradition bears the realization that Bohemia and Moravia will always only be strong with the Reich and always weak without the Reich.

Reinhard Heydrich

The Wenzels Tradition

At the ceremonial inspection of the coronation jewels in the Wenzels chapel, State President Dr. Hácha presented the seven keys and received back three of them for loyal hands to keep safe. This symbolic act ends centuries of despair and again marks the logic of the Führer's decisive deed of March 16, 1939.

This ceremony offers an opportunity to remember the Wenzels tradition in its full depth as well as to point out the historical significance of this region to the Reich in past, present and future. After most of the Germanic population moved away, other ethnic groups came to this region from the east, from which the present population developed in the course of centuries amid heavy mixture with the Germanic elements. In intellectual bearing and in political view, this advance was an east-west movement. In the course of the political and folkish development, the necessity of a clear relationship between the western and eastern neighbors quickly emerged. Initially, that resulted in a drive for independence and self-determination and led to a number of self-assertion conflicts with the bordering ethnic groups. Culturally, a separation from the east and approach to western concepts emerged. In diverse eras, geopolitical conditions necessitated the claim to help from the Reich against eastern and southeastern neighbors, which resulted in a reasonable subordination and integration into the Reich. From this time on the population of Bohemia and Moravia lived for centuries (also in terms of attitude) torn between east and west, namely the political dependence on and belonging to the Reich, and the drive for independence. Again and again throughout the history of Bohemia and Moravia and its inhabitants, manifestations played a role such as which we have seen emerge so fatefully in the past decades, yes in the last weeks and months. It was namely an unfortunate habit of these people, after military or political defeats, to bow their heads and swear allegiance, but to break their word and take their old path, if the

23

leadership of the Reich they had joined trusted their promise and militarily withdrew. Throughout history it was often the kings and rulers themselves who committed treason, sometimes it was their vassals who instigated revolt and treason against their rulers who remained loyal to the Reich leadership. In this sense, the fate of holy Wenzel and his brother/successor Boleslaus are a tragic example of this overall effect, but also a historical symbol for the clear political consequences for present and future. In recognition of historical necessary, Wenzel had totally joined the Reich and for the first time taken a position against the east. The rebels, under the leadership of his brother Boleslaus, opposed this. Misunderstanding the historical fate of this region and its eternal relationship to the Reich, although otherwise well-meaning, they purged Wenzel and his idea, murdered him, and under Boleslaus's leadership again attempted to be a bastion against the west. Back then, too, fate and region were stronger. Boleslaus himself, in the course of his experiences and events and after battles against the east, found the path back to the Reich. Hácha's decision in March 1939, which enabled the historically conclusive decision of the Führer, corresponds to the spirit of the genuine Wenzel tradition. The rebels against the Reich in those September-October days were not condemned solely because they failed to grasp this Wenzel tradition, but because beyond that - in a resurfacing of old eastern habits and breech of trust - they ambushed the Reich in order to again turn the bastion against the east into a bastion against the west. They forgot that the Reich's leadership had been warned by the experiences of history and was ready for the return of these symptoms. The Wenzel tradition bears the realization that Bohemia and Moravia will always only be great with the Reich and weak without the Reich. It also shows us, however, that the population – in consideration of the existence of many German ancestors - finally sees the obligation to draw the consequences from this historical realization in terms of inner attitude and education of their youth. And so the initial externality of this ceremonial act in the coronation chapel becomes a guideline for the population of Bohemia and Moravia in the spirit of the genuine Wenzel tradition.

Genuine leadership only has meaning and success, if people are won as co-workers, who then work together out of inner conviction on the common task for the Führer and the Reich.

Reinhard Heydrich

Speech to the Federation of German Girls, Work Service and War Assistance Service Maidens in the Rudolfinum in Prague on March 16, 1942

Girls and Maidens!

This evening you have shown in verse and song a representative sampling of what you are able to perform for the Führer and the German folk in the war. Many a spoiled child has worked in your community, learned to understand the meaning of work and become a proper, German girl.

Precisely on this militarily and historically significant soil of Bohemia and Moravia it seems correct to me to point out those principles whose inner realization is the prerequisite not only for your accomplishments, but also for the future of German youth itself.

In earlier times the youth was initially very superficial, fun-oriented and quite indifferent toward the problems regarding the future of folk and Reich. In the following time – especially in the times of the youth leagues – the youth's intellectual attitude twisted into the opposite, namely an arrogant sect. Today we strive for the goal to have a youth that, based on an inner, secure worldview, deals with the problems with youthful ease and youthful energy, without superficiality and without frivolity masters life with the goal of personal and objective accomplishment. The youth should look at the Reich's great problems seriously and consciously without thereby forgoing and forgetting the youthful gaiety and joy over the nearness of life, but at the same time not conversely exaggerate joy and thereby overlook the seriousness and necessity of the great problems. In short: It should be National Socialist in its inner life.

That is not expressed by always only talking about worldview and political problems, rather being a National Socialist is, in accordance with the Führer's example, a question of character.

The basic elements of education are conveyed through the youth leadership, the teacher and the parental home. However, in the young person's development they are deepened by correct self-recognition, by critical self-examination and finally by self-discipline. The basic ideas are again self-recognition, the bare and true recognition of one's own imperfections and the iron will to remove them and overcome oneself. The main ideas of education content are the uncompromising purity of German blood, the uncompromising drive for clarity of character, love of truth, modesty, pride that tolerates no arrogance, healthy ambition that demands highest accomplishment without egoism, and not last the drive for professional excellence.

For you girls and maidens, however, I want to add one thing: Despite all self-discipline and self-control, you should not march in step, militarize and harden. The most beautiful thing about a woman – and especially about a German woman – is the feminine, the womanly, which itself makes a woman beautiful. Guard your femininity during all your work and action. War denies a lot of joy to youth, too. You do not just participate in the mighty experience of Germandom's great times, rather you can also note with inner satisfaction that, already in your youth, you could help to create, build and fight for the Führer's work. Especially in this region, Bohemia and Moravia, that has been won back for the Reich governmentally and militarily - in this region, whether you are Germans from this region or you come from the Greater German Reich - you have a special task to fulfill as good examples, as convincing German people within the fighting German community. Whether you fulfill your task in the countryside, in an office, in the city, within the narrower German area or in contact with the Czech inhabitants of this land, always realize that a lot depends on the work and attitude of every single one of you and that this hence contributes a lot to the completion of the tasks the Führer has given all of us.

Everywhere you go and stand and work, you must be the bearers of the idea, be good examples of National Socialism in unshakeable faith in the Führer and in Germany. And so we now, together, want to jointly remember the man who builds the Reich's future especially for you, German youth, German girls and maidens, whom we owe everything: Adolf Hitler.

Music is the creative language of artistic and musical people as the conveyor of their inner life.

Reinhard Heydrich

On the Occasion of the Ceremony for the Reopening of the Rudolfinums in Prague as a German Culture Center on October 16, 1941

Party Comrades! Honored Guests!

As Deputy Reich Protector I today have the honor to complete with this state ceremony the architectural renewal of the Rudolfinums, which the now ill Reich Protector, Reich Minister Freiherr von Neurath, ordered on April 11, 1940 and which was announced at a party celebration on June 30th of the same year.

Allow me to first outline the history of this culture center in dates. This conveys the fateful development of this region during the past decades without romantic embellishment.

In 1872 the Bohemian Bank – back then a completely German institution – on the occasion of the 50th anniversary of its existence decided to "erect a building devoted to music, sculpture and applied arts".

Built between 1876 and 1884, this house of art was named after then Crown Prince Rudolf "Rudolfinum" on February 7, 1885 and officially opened. For 33 years the Rudolfinum served its original purpose:

The conduct of German concerts: men like Karl Much the still living Emil Nikolaus von Rezniczek started on their path from here. One of the greatest composers of those days, Anton Brückner, took over the organ built into the great concert hall.

It was home of the Prague Conservatory - founded in 1911 by the "Association for the Promotion of Music in Bohemia" – one of the oldest German music education institutions of this kind. And for the exhibit and collection of the "Society of Patriotic Patrons of Music" founded in 1796.

In October, right after formation of the unprecedented Czechoslovakian Republic, the "Assocation for the Promotion of Music" was forced to dissolve. The "Prague Conservatory" was Czechified and taken over by the state. The "Society of Patriotic Patrons of Music" also had to remove their art collection from the building. The first session of the Czech parliament occurred on May 26, 1920.

On December 15, 1921 the "Bohemian Bank" had to sell the building to the Czech state. The great concert hall was remodeled into the delegation house and the organ there was moved to to the stadium hall in Brunn. The organ bench where Anton Bruckner had sat was smashed with an axe in order to make space for a bust of Masaryk.

On December 16, 1938 the parliament held its last session. And today we are solemnly united in order to finally consecrate this place of German art. At this moment I hereby state the obligations!

For the artists: to always be German artists in the sense of the Reich.

For us leaders: to always pave the way for the productive and the creative people of art, to give them the mental and material prerequisites for productivity free of daily concerns.

In this sense, I will tomorrow at the castle bestow the "Prize of the Reich Protector 1941" on three German artists as reward, incentive and aid.

Now let us briefly examine the basics of the life of folks in regard to the reciprocal action anchored within them, and especially reciprocal action between art and politics and race as well as the soul and heart of the people of our folk.

Historical times of true greatness and inner contact always produce a blossoming time of true art and genuine ability. Historically and politically WEAK times let folks nourish themselves from the art of the greats of their time and gain strength to overcome political decline. At the same time the triumph of a few genius strengthen the impulses for new POLITICAL LIFE. APPARENT blossoming times (in the political sense) such as the end of the 19th century usually also produce an APPARENT blossoming time in the art, because the deception and the superficiality of political business is carried over in the art. In periods of cultural and worldwide decline and rapid political change an artist all too easily saves himself in superficial form:

The POET in over-exaggeration of the language's eloquence, the composer in the strictness of the laws of composition or in comfortable, light music.

The architect, sculptor and painter in expressionism. Out of material need they unfortunately very often drift into dependency on the constantly changing political parties. The JEW has recognized this danger in HIS sense. He has intensified it and increasingly alienated art and culture from the folk, the race, the heart and the soul of the folk. In this region of Bohemia and Moravia, eternally and fatefully bound to the Reich, the Jew has coupled this de-politicalization of art with a total false tribal hatred. He has injected Czechdom with the insanity of sovereignty and blinded it to centuries of political experience with their natural integration into the Reich. Finally, he tried to turn King Wenzel – who in reality always recognized and affirmed the deeper meaning of Reich membership – into a holy symbol against the Reich and the Reich's culture. When as Reich Deputy Protector I return this home of art to German culture, I thereby turn in all seriousness to all artists and creative people with the admonishment that they form their works as Germans from innermost worldview faith, with whole heart and pure character. Masters with their works are not individual figures without blood and homeland, rather people who, consciously or not, draw their energy from the feeling of their folk and the fate of their region.

May you all have as an eternal example the greatest artist and shaper, the greatest German: Adolf Hitler!

Address at the German Rally in the Prague Opera House on March 15, 1942

Today's ceremony hat united us for two ideas: Remembrance of the Führer's decisive three years ago that is so fateful for the Reich and for Bohemia-Moravia - and to express gratitude to the fallen heroes.

Precisely in difficult times rich in sacrifice German history and the heroism of those who form it demand that we do not celebrate these days of remembrance in a narrow and petty fashion, but instead always prove ourselves worthy of the genuine greatness. In this sense this celebration is for us an hour of looking back, of reflection, of consolidation and looking, of both a historical and a human kind. Historically, we want to look back at the recent past of the Reich's decline and discord which as always – even when viewed long-term – means times of need and weakness for this region and its people. We want to look back farther, but again and again bring to mind our Reich's successes and mistakes and keep them awake within ourselves as an eternal admonishment for the future.

Whether it was the time of the consolidation of Germandom or the struggle between Kaiser and Pope or the time when - allegedly for the good of the faith - the German folk almost bled dry in the Thirty Years War or the last World War or the National Socialist period of struggle - Germany was always in danger when it was disunited, mislead by aliens and tearing itself apart. But Germany was always victorious and great when it found faith in itself, its strength and its superiority - without losing a clear sense for reality and the recognition and elimination of its own mistakes. The holy faith in the strength Providence gave our folk has always overcome difficult times; cool reason and boundless will put the leadership in the position to rationally master the dangers.

Viewed historically, March 15, 1938 is not just the fulfillment of the wishes of the German heart, rather rationally and logically the real completion of a political necessity.

The great war we now experience is the life-decisive struggle for the existence of Greater Germany and Europe. Precisely because of its necessary sacrifice and burden it will contribute politically, economically and humanly as a crucible to promote and complete the growth of this region into the Reich. So the present day, viewed politically, is a day of thankful and respectful memory of that March 15, 1939 that created the governmental and legal basis and the start for that development una those tasks that we want, together with the inhabitants of Bohemia and Moravia, to push ahead in the sense of the Reich and to complete according to the Führer's instructions.

Looking ahead, precisely in its connection to the remembrance of heroes this day carries a human obligation for each individual among us. Those fallen comrades have through the sacrifice of their life directed an obligating admonishment to each of us living to tirelessly stand our ground particularly in those moments and times of fighting and spiritual burdens and to bravely overcome the little burdens of every day life in the homeland. Despondency slyly sneaks into the hearts of many people from time to time. Precisely then, we must again and again find inner strength within ourselves in the thought of our heroes and in the faith in our beloved Führer, live fighting and employing all energy for victory, for the Führer and for Germany.

After stern measures that have become necessary, it is much easier to be just and humane than would have been allowed by constant compromises, which are simply interpreted as weakness and hence often lead to insubordination.

Reinhard Heydrich

Walter Wannenmacher

Reinhard Heydrich

Politics stands between art and strategy. Politics has in common with strategy the planning of path and goal and the selection of the corresponding means for the achievement of the planning will. Elements of strategic planing and strategic means are essentially abstract in nature; strategy thinks in numbers that signify troop units, elevation differences, transport capacities, fire-power, supply requirements and other things. Aside from one exception, namely the spirit of the troop, it deals with exact concepts, and even the incalculable influences of enemy action and weather can be dealt with in maximum and minimum factors. However, since politics represents the influencing of relationships of groups of people directed by will, be they folks, parties or other formations, their planing and their means lack exact elements. Politics works in the sphere of human will-formation, hence where feelings usually have more weight than logical considerations. Hence instincts are also the decisive advisor in political planning and selection of means, because abstract reason alone is often helpless against the rationally incomprehensible secrets of the will-formation of a group of people, even more helpless than the psychologist researching the secrets of the mass will and the individual will. Insofar as it comes down to creative instinct, politics is related to art. With instinctive certainty the artist creates the beauty and the politician creates the suggestive. The former appeals to people as recipients of impressions; the latter appeals to people as will-bearers. Standing between art and strategy, politics requires cool reason as well as life-warm instinct. So it is no coincidence that great politicians at the same time always have something musical and something military about them.

The realization is necessary in order to comprehend the political work that a man of military and musical bend starts in Prague, but can not finish:

Reinhard Heydrich. He immediately recognized his goal: to positively direct the will of the inhabitants of the Bohemian-Moravian region to the Reich idea. His creative instinct simultaneously found the path and the means as well. Since every political will-formation is somehow bound to legacy, he studied the region's history and found in the mission of the Bohemian King Wenzel the historical basis for the new Reich idea. At the same time he saw in Palacky's hate-distorted view of history that hostile cell that had spread its seductive and dangerously poisonous spores under Bensch in the twenty years after the First World War. There could be no doubt about the foggy effect of the narcotics that had flourished in the most recent past influenced by Palackey. They showed themselves in diverse ways: in the apparently apathetic, indifferent attitude of leading personalities and in the furious sabotage acts of agitated or paid lackeys, in open and in hidden resistance, in omissions that were often as serious as hostile actions. Heydrich realized that these groups represented a minority of the Czech folk, but a dangerous minority, because the tendency for romantic-megalomaniac illusions was widespread in this region since 1918, and the susceptibility for infection of this kind had to be estimated high. Benesch had been paid by the English precisely for the spread of this disease, because the more people infected, the easier to find more people for sabotage for the purpose of the British sniper strategy. Openly a quick operative action could prevent the spread of the disease. Back then the Czechs still did not imagine what hesitation would have meant for them. The person acts humanely who, after conscientious research of all possibilities, does what is necessary with minimum sacrifice. Any delay of the action would have meant greater spread of the disease and also reduced the chances of the operation's success. Yes, a long delay could have only ended with a complete catastrophe for the Czech folk. It was humane to avert this catastrophe in time, and because this would sooner or later be realized by the Czechs, it was decided to eliminate it with the successful surgeon.

Heydrich's measures against saboteurs and swindlers were designed to protect the Czech folk; first against exploitation as a British tool by ruthlessly exposing the danger of flirting with Benesch illusions and proving that such flirting could only lead to a bad end; second against material exploitation by people who, in their greed for personal enrichment, often also put on the halo of disruptor of proper supply.

The operative incision had to be followed by a period of healing. Heydrich realized there was only one medicine for the seduction of romantic narcotics: common sense. Starting with the Wenzel tradition with its memory of the prosperity in the Bohemian lands, he employed the persuasive power of common sense as a political tool. If the Czechs could calmly obey healthy reason, they would have to see that they had every reason to be satisfied with their fate; this fate protected them against war, hunger and destruction, and it demanded no blood sacrifice from them, rather just work, indeed well-paid work. Not love for the Reich, rather just some reason and gratitude, expressed in active cooperation with the overall European tasks in their own interest, was demanded from them. So Heydrich approached his constructive task closely bound to life's reality. He received workers and peasants, he improved supply and he saw to it that the working man could be appropriately paid, fed and clothed, insofar as this appeared possible under the war conditions. Recreational areas for workers with many children were created and work shoes were distributed for free. After reformation of the Protectorate government an administrative reform was launched, the concept of a service obligation for Czech youth emerged based on the idea that youth should not grow up in boredom and without leadership, if useful and decent people are desired. The politician Reinhard Heydrich was always conscious that the will formation of a group of people - if disturbed by narcotic-induced emotions - can only be brought back into balance through the persuasive power of healthy reason; this reason has nothing to do with the hair-splitting intellect of an infertile stratum of "educated people". However, he also appreciated the feeling of security that stems from a clear course in politics as the real root of any authority. So the passengers, whether sympathetic or antagonistic, can always view the man at the helm with the same calm demeanor on the correctly plotted course, without that tactical maneuvering often erroneously viewed by small spirits as the essence of politics. They all soon started to feel that the man at the helm knew exactly where he wanted to go, and that his will would prevail. Providence decided otherwise. The murderers who extinguished the life of one of the mightiest political figures of the Greater German Reich in his prime could not, however, extinguish the name that signifies path and goal in this region. Reinhard Heydrich's work will live on, born by all those who today stand shaken under the spell of the tragedy of his death.

A clear guideline for the future: do everything that serves a Europe led by Greater Germany, and avoid and combat what harms it.

Reinhard Heydrich, September 8, 1941

We see our task in the motto: "Opponent of all enemies and protector of everything German.'

Reinhard Heydrich

II.
The Changes
of Our Struggle

Changes of the Forms of Struggle

As everywhere in nature, the life of folks consists *of eternal struggle* between the stronger, nobler, racially superior and lower sub-humanity. The way this struggle is fought, however, is subject to constant change. The form of struggle is above all dependent on who has the upper hand at the time.

Our Führer's and the movement's struggle began in a time period of the disguised rule by sub-humanity, which was in the process, through Bolshevism, of gaining open power and brutally destroying everything. *This enemy could not be defeated outside the state.* An inner reconstruction of state and folk from the outside was hardly possible. So the Führer gave his following the first immediate objective: "Achievement of *eternal state* power."

The means for that were hence *necessarily* those of the opponent and initially relatively external: elections, assemblies, organizing the masses – indeed organizing them more firmly that the opponent did.

The party itself as the motor of this elective following was a devote community of men with the same direction and spirit. The faith was directed at the achievement of the immediate goal set by the Führer and the related defeat of the visible parts of the opponent, his organizational assets, his party, his trade unions etc..

Since the tempo of the struggle against this well-prepared opponent was tremendously swift, the fighting community of the party had *little time to comprehend the worldview proclaimed by the Führer in its full depth and to convey it to the always newly arriving comrades.*

When the immediate goal was suddenly achieved, it seemed to most comrades that the opponents had simply disappeared with the destruction of the hostile organizations. They sought him, but no longerfound him, because he for the most part conformed. A condition set in that, unfortunately, still applies to many: Unable to find the opponent in his new positions, they waste their energy in senseless, lineless personal illegalities. They thus harm the Führer's idea and at the same time show that they are far from comprehending the tremendous greatness of the idea itself and the tasks related to it.

They have in reality, unfortunately, only seen and fought the opposing political *parties*. They do not see that these parties were only the external manifestations, optimized for the situation at the time, of spiritual forces that fought Germany by fighting the Führer and the NSDAP, that want to exterminate Germany along

with all of its strong forces of blood, spirit and soil.

The same movement comrades naturally remained loyal to the Führer in the years of struggle before the rise to power, they followed him faithfully, despite the fact, or because of it, that the opponent dissolved National Socialist organizations, banned its newspaper and took away the uniforms. All of them unconsciously felt that the power of the state back then was ineffective in its opposition against the their faith and *their worldview, spiritual bearing.* And now, when the forms of struggle experience changes, because the opponent's organizations have been destroyed, *they no longer remember their own experiences.*

Every organization is nothing without the forces that give spirit to its ideas.

If the opponent's organizations are now destroyed or at least in the process of reorganization, then for us that only means that the form of struggle changes. The opponent's driving forces remain eternally the same: World Jewry, World Freemasonry and a largely political clerical officialdom that misuses religion. In their widely dispersed branches and forms they persist in their goal of destruction of our folk with its blood, spirit and soil bound strengths.

It is necessary that we realize that the struggle has become *deeper. It can no longer be waged solely with technical means.*

We must learn to recognize the opponent from the history of the *last millennia.* We will then suddenly see that we today, for the first time, seize the opponent at the roots of his power. Is it any wonder that he resists so bitterly? That he *tries to use all the tricks from his centuries of combat experience?*

We must realize that these opponents can not be eliminated solely by the external takeover of the state apparatus, for they sit with their cross-connections in all branches of our folk life and the state structure. We must calmly ascertain that up to the last years the opponent was well on his way to systematically undermine German man in character and spirit, to poison him and to leave him only his Nordic face.

We fighters must come to this realization: We need years of bitter fighting in order to finally push back the opponent in all areas, to annihilate him and to secure Germany in blood and spirit against the opponent's new penetrations.

Unfortunately, even among us in the S.S. there are many who are often not conscious of this great, long-term goal. When, after the rise to power, everything *visibly* hostile had disappeared, when the *strug-*

gle of spirits began, the lack of recognition of the comprehensive extent of the opponent also meant lack of mental equipment.

It will be explained to them in the following pages that the prerequisite for the successful continuation and completion of the struggle are two things:

The correction recognition of the opponent in his deepest essence and the uniform view of our own tasks, as well as our own mistakes, with all the prerequisites and conclusions.

As in every genuine struggle there are very clearly only two possibilities: *"Either we utterly overcome the opponent or we perish."*

II. The Visible Opponent

It must be stated right off that the opponent can not be exhaustively covered here. It can only deal with suggestions and indications that should sharpen the eye for the opponent.

In order to be able to overcome him, one must learn to recognize his *changing* appearances and his means of struggle. We must not allow ourselves to be deceived about his precise evaluation by the numerousness of the apparently feuding groups with their divergent programs. All of them are only clever subordinate or parallel branches of the great opponents. They are intended to serve as advance posts or as collection organizations. When, therefore, Freemasonry was mentioned after Jewry, it was *only done for the sake of better understanding.* In truth Freemasonry is a service organization of Jewry, so that in the final analysis we only have to view *the Jews and the political clerics* (in their most pronounced form called *"Jesuits"*) as the foundation of all groups of opponents.

These opponents sometimes wage their struggle in visible, tangible form and other times in camouflaged and not directly visible form. Let us first cover in broad outlines the visible activity of the opponent.

a) Political Misuse of the Churches

Above all, we must recognize in time the anti-state and anti-folk intentions and effects of the fighting between the religious denominations, whose location is again Germany. *Originally, the churches were supposed to be serving mediators between God and men.* As the founders proclaimed, the kingdom of the churches "is not of this earth".

A totally political and worldly ambitious clerical officialdom, however, has bent their founder's teachings. All of them today claim today that precisely *they and their church alone* have God's power of attorney for this mediator role. Independent from whether or not they had justification for this claim, all of them derive their *worldly* political action from *this* power of attorney. It is not enough that they have worked for centuries to destroy our folk's values of blood and spirit, the fake through adoption of external forms the preservation of these values and today claim they are the guardians of these values. *Instead of being truly selfless mediators, under the pretext of church affairs they conquer one worldly power position after the other.*

In order, however, to secure and reinforce these worldly positions, the church's followers were organized politically. Before the rise to power, the politically worldly character found clear expression in the pure form of political parties (Centrum, Bavarian Folk Party). Today many clubs etc., founded earlier in wise anticipation to serve as collection organizations, *have become the successors of the parties* (Catholic Union etc.). With clerical embellishment, the political infiltration of all areas of our folk life is here demanded and sought. While Germany's clerical press denies the political character of these organizations, *the foreign voices of the same churches openly admit it.* The best example for this usurpation of a worldly kind is probably the position of the churches and the attempt of sabotage against the sterilization law and race legislation. In order to expand their worldly sphere of influence, the clerical schooling of non-priests, so-called laymen, greatly intensified after the rise to power. In hundreds of drill houses, they were "drilled", as the name fittingly says. That means everything had to be mechanized as much as possible, so that the people involved do not notice how all their inherited strengths of blood and spirit are systematically twisted or deadened.

In National Socialism the Führer has after centuries finally achieved unification in *one* great community. That was only possible, because in National Socialism he *again resurrected the hereditary foundations of our folk.* The worldly ambition of the political clergy had not reckoned with that. However, since an open political or social schism was not possible in order to save their position, the old denominational conflict had to suddenly come back to life under the slogan: *"The denominations are in danger".* So that is how one inserts mistrust and doubt into the folk community united by the Führer, and tries to sow discord in party and state.

Allegedly, this fight is waged against godlessness for the salvation of Christian virtues and for the preservation of "German" culture. But if one views the *political* leadership corps of clerics – from whom the faithful follower of his church expects a good example of these "endangered" virtues as self-evident – then one must ascertain with disappointment *that these prerequisites do not exist.*

On the contrary, mountains of documents show how false is the moral and cultural foundation of this leadership corps as well as the motto of its fight. In truth they fight not for the positive preservation of religious and cultural values (that are not in any danger), rather they continue their embittered struggle for worldly domination of Germany.

b) Jewry

The Jew was always the mortal enemy of all Nordic-led and racially healthy folks. His goal was and remains the world rule by a more or less visible Jewish upper stratum. For the achievement of his goal *every* means and *every* organization form is fine to him, even if they may look ever so dumb and ridiculous on the outside. *The path always remains the same.*

Every folk that in times of political and racial weakness allows the immigration and above all the later racial mixing with Jews was systematically undermined. The undermining of the blood had next to the racial bastardization a slow blurring of the distinct race idea of the "host folk" as a result. A gradual penetration of all areas of folk life and a systematic spiritual poisoning thus became possible. So, for example, in the Middle Ages in England and by us did the guilds and stone masons, through complete permeation with Jewish ways and Jewish basic elements, get turned into purely Jewish Freemasonry.

While Jewry in earlier centuries conquered the key positions at the princes' courts such as treasurer and political advisor (who were often camouflaged as court jester), until the World War the noble, for the most part racially solid German upper stratum was undermined. Skillful money-marriages and, unfortunately, the granting by too many German princes of nobility status to their Jewish money-lenders, bastardized the upper strata, not yet completely pushed out of leadership, so much, that Jewish-developed and Jewish-led Marxist and Bolshevik revolts could easily overcome them.

After the rise to power race legislation has indeed greatly restricted Jewry's *direct* influence. The Jew, however, in his tenacity and ambition, only sees this as a *restriction*. For him there are initially only the questions: How can the old position be won back, and how can I work to hurt Germany?

In evaluation of manner of struggle one must distinguish between *Jewish organizations* that openly work as Jews and the *auxilliary formations* that are led by Jewish world organizations.

The Jews living inside Germany fall into two groups, the *Zionists and the assimilationists* (who characteristically call themselves German-Jews). The Zionists do indeed take a strong racialist standpoint and strive, through emigration to Palestine, for the creation of their own Jewish state, but one must not let oneself be deceived about the fundamentally anti-folkish position of the Jews. The assimilationists deny their Jewish race by emphasizing their long stay and claiming to be either *Germans* or after baptism *Christians*. The assimilationists who above all use all kinds of declarations of loyalty as well as the pushiness characteristic of their race to try to ruin all National Socialist principles.

They also tried to make use of the introduction of compulsory military service. Associations led by former, retired officers (Reich Federation of Jewish Front Soldiers and Association of National-German Jews), after introduction of the new law, did not fail to try to achieve the inclusion of Jews in the armed forces.

Although the individual Jew, who has no interest at all in German military duty, shows no inclination to voluntarily accept the demands of the soldier's life, he was pushed by the sharp action of the association leaders toward voluntary enlistment for the sake of political goals.

While here, for the sake of breaking the Aryan legislation, the Jew disguised himself as extremely patriotic, the Jewish wave of boycotts rolls on unabated as well as the foreign press campaign against Germany led by Jewish emigrants.

The *Freemason lodges* and their related organizations, which likewise stand under Jewish leadership, only have the purpose to organize people in apparently harmless social form and to make them usable for Jewry's purposes. *There are corresponding branches for all state forms and occupations.* Regardless who governs, one form of their lodge fits the state form of the moment. In times of liberalism and democracy the *humanitarian* lodges stood on the foreground, and in times of *nationalist* governments the so-called nationalist lodges. If Bolshevism had broken through, *worker lodges* would been dominant.

The methods for making stupid and dominating people are strangely similar in the drill houses of clerical officialdom. It is tried, through the most diverse exercises of this mechanization, to deaden and twist one racially German and spiritual characteristic *after another*. Upon acceptance into the higher grades a blind submission, *undisturbed by any racial instinct,* is assured.

Beyond this, in the lodges – in crass contrast to the obvious principles of healthy folk and state life – blind subordination to *unknown and secret* superiors is demanded. This obedience is reinforced with an oath framed with gruesome Jewish customs.

That *Bolshevism* is one of the most important creations of Jewry, will hopefully be understood by even the most forgetful citizen due to the experiences of the past years and decades. Covering its danger is probably superfluous here.

The Aryan legislation does not banish Jewry's danger to Germany.

The Jewish auxilliary organizations with all the connections to their international leadership work now as in the past for the destruction of our folk with all of its values. All the branches of our folk life like art, science, economics etc., which the Jew had almost fully permeated with his ideas, are as a result of the achievement of necessary short-term goals still far from being free of the enemy. *Here are the hidden paths upon which, in millions of channels, he tries to expand his sphere of influence step by step.*

His work is made easier for him because there are still folk comrades (the churches even promote this attitude) who accept the Aryan legislation openly under compulsion and do not want to comprehend the fundamental racial ideas.

While one portion of the German folk now already two years after the National Socialist revolution begins to become indifferent toward the Jew, we see on the Jewish side a stubborn, eternally constant striving for his goal, which is always: *world domination and the destruction of the Nordic folks.*

III. The Camouflaged Opponent

In contrast to the visible opponent, the camouflaged opponent is *not organizationally tangible.* He works illegally; we can perhaps call him the invisible apparatus of the already mentioned great opponents. His goal is to destroy the unity of the leadership in state and party in order to make the achievement of National Socialism's worldview tasks impossible. The folk is supposed to become reserved and unsure of the leadership; the leaders are supposed to become nervous and mutually distrustful.

For this purpose there exists a *net of cross-connections* to almost all offices of the state apparatus, of public life and of the movement. On the one hand, this channel system informs the opponent about the danger that awaits him. So he learns in time about all state measures, regulations and laws. On the other hand, the same channel system also serves the task of preparing the countermeasures important to the opponent.

In part, the organs of this channel system consciously work treasonously; in part, their personal weaknesses are *unconsciously* misused.

The main supports of this opposing, consciously treasonous work are a *few hostile elements still remaining* in the state apparatus who, *pretending to be 110%,* immediately conformed. The state official act passed them by. Believing in the sincerity of their loud declarations of loyalty, they were kept in their positions as *experts.*

While we National Socialists view bureaucracy in the positive sense as the concept of the perfect precision of the splendid and smoothly working of a business and administrative apparatus, these soulless and hostile elements misuse the same bureaucracy for hindrance, retardment and detour of our National Socialist tasks.

The branching of his net is enormous. A complete listing is impossible here. The layman can recognize the branching only through the effects:

Here attempts were made to circumvent legislative measures.

There it was attempted to cut off financing for a range of tasks vital to movement and state.

In *institutions of higher learning* it is tried, through "purely scientific and objective" treatment, to bend National Socialist ideas in favor of liberalism.

In archeological research it is attempted to put one-sided, un-folkish elements in charge of excavations in order to still safely prop up the claim that our ancestors were "uncultured".

Through the attempt of anti-National Socialist *personnel policy*, the regaining of key positions in the state is sought, so that, if a National Socialist law goes through, the execution can be sabotaged and back doors can be opened through compliance regulations. The attempt is made to gain influence with good National Socialist men through social ties (invitations, clubs etc.). They twist the burning desire of National Socialist superiors - to adapt National Socialist legislation and German administration to the nature and feeling of the folk - in its application and thereby try to put these National Socialist men in opposition to the movement.

In order to bend a measure of the Führer or one of his representatives, or to bring down uncomfortable and dangerous organizations of the movement, they make use of the means of systematic spreading of rumours and press agitation. Through thousands of channels the leading offices are quietly warned what "dangers" to the Führer's politics are posed by these measures or these organizations, and at the same time a flood of complaints sets in. *The diversity of these complaints often makes the opponents channel system immediately recognizable.*

At the command of usually a Swiss Freemason or "German" emigrant newspaper, the attack is completed with an artillery barrage of lies. *At the same moment* the apparatus for exploitation of character weaknesses of individual men inside the movement in set in motion. People tend all too readily to believe untrue and believable rumours instead of objective facts. In realization of these weaknesses and people's rumour-mongering the rumours are taken to personalities who have certain sympathy or dislike for these organizations who then themselves ensure the further dissemination in either positive or negative sense.

All too quickly a pre-fabricated opinion is produced, which then forms the basis for the fulfilment of the opponent's immediate goals.

So it is gradually tried to undermine the state's framework and to drive a wedge between leadership and following. By stressing the not yet completed tasks the deeds and accomplishments of the first two years are supposed to be forgotten, and the Führer and his loyal followers are gradually supposed to gradually be denied the basis for any positive work – *the trust of the folk.*

We must see this work and tactic of the opponent in order to be able to counter it.

How the *opponent wants to see* the situation in Germany and what path seems right for him, may be shown by the following sentence from a secret enemy report:

"The situation in Germany is characterized by the NSDAP's attempt for standardization through bureaucracy and other secret opponents of National Socialism."

IV. Our Task

The recognition of the opponent was discussed as *one* great prerequisite of the struggle. We now know his goal, his changing methods and his new manifestations.

What necessities are required of us, the movement, in order to deal with these changes of the struggle?

First, we must realize that the state apparatus, the State Police in particular, can not wage this struggle *alone*. The police can only counter the external, juristically tangible form of the opponent's anti-state attitude and is hence more an organ of defense. Worldview opponents can only be decisively defeated in the spiritual struggle by the *worldview*. After the first months of the revolutionary conquest of state power the standardizations were hence halted. When many comrades failed to realize the necessary change of the struggle, the expression "from revolution to evolution" was coined, from the externally conquered position of power to the spiritual and worldview winning of all.

What demand does this new chapter of struggle place on us, the SS?

We must work on ourselves. Through ceaseless self-discipline, we must anchor and secure in ourselves the eternal principles of the worldview given us by the Führer. We must first standardize ourselves spiritually, so each thinks the same about the opponent, equally rejects him without making personally egocentric and sympathetic exceptions. In order to preserve our folk, we must be very hard toward the opponent, even at the risk of sometimes hurting an individual opponent as a human or appearing to many certainly well meaning people to be undisciplined brutes. If we do not fulfill our historical task as National Socialists, because we are too objective and humane, one will nonetheless not grant us moderating circumstances. It will only be said: They did not fulfill their task before history. If somebody is our conscious opponent, he must be defeated subjectively and without exception. If for ex-

ample every German out of pity excludes even just "one decent" Jew or Freemason from the fight, that would mean 60 million exceptions.

The work on ourselves must proceed in terms of *character* and *performance.* We must deepen the good elements of our German genes. Despite all hardness, we must be *just,* we must be the most loyal, and there must be no better comradeship than our own. We must purge the harmful and shortcomings within our own ranks with possibly even greater hardness. In order to prove the correctness of the principles of our community and our selection, we must gradually become the best in all areas. **We must in connection with military service present the best recruits to the weapons bearer of the nation; in sports we must always be among the first. In the professions, too, it should become a rule that the consciously political SS-man is also the best expert, in tests as well as in practice. Through our** *accomplishment* **we must make the purely** *"non-political"* **expert (who is nothing more that) dispensable.**

We must also expand our knowledge of our ancestors or even first acquire it. It is knowledge of all the values that God has given our folk: Our blood, our kind, our true historical past. That includes our ancient folk, which - contrary to the claims of many - has its roots far before the time of Christ and far before the - for Germandom so important - 8th century.

We must provide an exemplary living example of the eternal principles provided by the Führer and in positive form try to win over in terms of worldview the people who in the first months due to their character and attitude did not want to go along with an external standardization. All those people who could not find the idea's content due to a faux pas, we must try to win over, personally, man by man, through our accomplishments and the strength of faith that we as the National Socialist movement are allowed to be the smallest link between the high cultural past of our folk and future millennia of German-folkish history.

And we, the SS, want to thereby be the worldview assault troop and the guardian of the Führer's idea, and at the same time, in the fulfillment of the State Police's tasks, insofar as we serve in it, the inner-political protection corps of the National Socialist state.

III.
Eulogies to the National Socialist Reinhard Heydrich

Reichsleiter Martin Bormann, Head of the Party Chancellory

Reinhard Heydrich's towering achievement for the National Socialist movement is the Security Service! Early and quickly, the Reichsführer-SS had recognized Heydrich's special abilities: Already in 1931 he assigned him this difficult, special area! The right man was hence at the right place. Only an unblemished National Socialist, a man of great energy, a man with sure and clear judgement would be able to master the assigned task. With penetrating reason and infallible instinct, Reinhard Heydrich differentiated between the apparently genuine, from the human-all-too-human and the really bad. Again and again, his clear reason and infallible instinct proved themselves by uncovering and pursuing the enemies of party and state. In the really shortest time Heydrich always pondered all his opponent's possibilities, spread them out like a fan in front of the Reichsführer-SS, and could usually report the completion of assignment and task within the shortest time.

Just how carefully and thoroughly Reinhard Heydrich worked, what comprehension foundations he gave to his office's work, can only be measured by whoever could repeatedly observe the activity of the Reich Security Main Office on the spot. Tirelessly and with an almost unbelievable industriousness, Reinhard Heydrich worked on the perfection of this instrument; he had recognized the greatness of the overall task to be mastered and hence also the greatness of the task assigned to him! He saw that the Führer allowed himself no rest; and hence he, too, enjoyed neither satisfied comfort nor carefree rest, rather his creative spirit worked without rest.

By all his really difficult work Reinhard Heydrich always remained a happy, strong optimist. How much human weakness, inadequacy and badness did he see! Nonetheless, he always remained the unworried, aggressive National Socialist, whose faith in the mastery of the tasks simply could not be shaken!

In the context of his assignment Heydrich at first faced the task to research the spiritual foundations and international connections of all the opponents of the movement, in order to combat them on the basis of acquired knowledge. He was here not solely concerned with the preservation of external state security, rather especially with the protection of the National Socialist movement and worldview. He clearly recognized that combating the opponents could only be a partial task within the development of the National Socialist Greater German Reich; he knew that the nation's existence could only be secured in the long-run, if the opponents were struck at their spiritual roots by the National Socialist movement, and if the positive work of the party led to the worldview unity of the German folk.

Reinhard Heydrich created a security corps that, in crass contrast to the institutions of other states, watched over the Reich's security in all openness and rigor as a worldview battle troop. Each member of the SD was to be so solid in worldview and character, that he could fulfill this difficult and often thankless task without suffering harm as a human being. The laws of the SS provided the prerequisites for this. It was possible to put young party forces from the most diverse occupations to work in the SD. Much young talent was thereby drawn into responsible cooperation that would not have been fully possible on the path of a normal career precisely during the decisive years of development. What was accomplished by these coworkers, often in silence without any external recognition, is exemplary even in the history of the party so rich in voluntary service. Heydrich demanded the highest performance from his men, and therefore he achieved sifting and training of a leadership corps that will continue the assigned tasks in his spirit.

The Security Service of the Reichsführer-SS, which has the task of acquiring and processing of intelligence material for the party, became the political information and counterintelligence service of the party, its auxilliaries and associated groups. As an institution of the party the SD hence supplied the foundation for a comprehension exchange of experiences. The SD did not limit itself to the instruction of the leadership offices about hostile efforts, rather it instructed beyond that, continuously and extensively, about the development and misdevelopment in all work areas of folk life. This systematic work of the Security Service in all life areas provided the possibility to bring wishes and suggestions from all parts of the Reich and all population strata to the direct knowledge of the highest Reich offices. Beyond that, a number of positive suggestions for the party's work grew from the SD's sifting work.

Whoever worked with SS-Obergruppenführer Heydrich again and again found much pleasure in his athletic-soldierly bearing, his extensive knowledge and his sure judgement.

He always kept with unerring hardness to the line he recognized as worldview to be right! As flexible as his methods were, so tenacious and stubborn did his National Socialist bearing remain. Acceptance of his tasks meant restless devotion to him!

The NSDAP lost one of its best in Reinhard Heydrich!

We must work on ourselves. Through ceaseless self-discipline, we must anchor and secure in ourselves the eternal principles of the worldview given us by the Führer. We must first standardize ourselves spiritually, so each thinks the same about the opponent, equally rejects him without making personally egocentric and sympathetic exceptions. In order to preserve our folk, we must be very hard toward the opponent, even at the risk of sometimes hurting an individual opponent as a human or appearing to many certainly well meaning people to be undisciplined brutes. If we do not fulfill our historical task as National Socialists, because we are too objective and humane, one will nonetheless not grant us moderating circumstances. It will only be said: They did not fulfill their task before history.

The work on ourselves must proceed in terms of character and performance. We must deepen the good elements of our German genes. Despite all hardness, we must be just, we must be the most loyal, and there must be no better comradeship than our own. We must purge the harmful and shortcomings within our own ranks with possibly even greater hardness. We must also expand our knowledge of our ancestors or even first acquire it. It is knowledge of all the values that God has given our folk: Our blood, our kind, our true historical past. That includes our ancient folk, which - contrary to the claims of many - has its roots far before the time of Christ and far before the - for Germandom so important - 8th century.

We must provide an exemplary living example of the eternal principles provided by the Führer.

We, the SS, want to thereby be the worldview assault troop and the guardian of the Führer's idea, and at the same time, in the fulfillment of the State Police's tasks, insofar as we serve in it, the inner-political protection corps of the National Socialist state.

SS-Obergruppenführer Reinhard Heydrich

Secret State Police, Criminal Police and Security Service are still shrouded with the whispering secrecy of the crime novel. With a mixture of fear and creepiness, but inside the country still with a certain sense of security thanks to their existence, abroad one likes to attribute to the men of this work brutality, inhumanity bordering on sadism and heartlessness. Here one thinks there is nothing, right down to the smallest egotistical wish that cannot be provided by the Secret State Police. So, put humorously, we vary from a "maid-for-all-work" to the "trash can of the Reich".

However, whoever takes the effort to see the real work and seek the human beings in the men who work here, will ascertain with amazement that after painstaking, dreary and difficult training, clear worldview National Socialists stand here, who - in a fortunate combination of experienced practicians, painstaking and logically working scientists, fighting political soldiers and decent, understanding men — master their task in warm love for the Führer and fatherland.

Aside from providing many men for pure military service in the armed forces at the front, comes the security police work in connection with the army, for a small part as Secret Field Police, but for the most part as special security police action units with the goal of the political security of occupied territories. Naturally, all tasks here are multiplied by the fact that a supportive populace is lacking; it is either indifferent or, depending on the country's attitude, hostile. All that means a great reduction of the available work force within the Reich and an inconceivable, heightened demand on each individual performance. The work of the man of the Secret State Police and the Security Service is qualitatively determined, constant, still individual performance with a hardly believable, small number of exceptional men. Always on solitary duty, qualitative excellence is demanded, but also performed.

An important fact makes things harder for these men - in contrast to the men who stand at the front in the armed forces -, aside from the joy to be allowed armed front service: the work. The soldierly, manly deed of front soldiers, due to the speed of operations, can be very quickly crowned with public recognition, decoration and success. The political soldier of the "secret front", on the other man, must be silent, incredibly patient, often only serving other political factors, and work in the certainty that his deed only much later, many times never, will be publicly recognized.

The Security Police and the Security Service stand their ground in accordance with the Führer's instructions under the command of their Reichsführer-SS. They only want one thing: to work and fight for Germany.

SS-Obergruppenführer Reinhard Heydrich on the Day of the German Police in 1941

SS-Oberst-Gruppenführer Daluege

In the spirit of political soldiery he led his SS-men in the strictest discipline to be as severe as the safety of the whole required, but never more severe than the overall fate of the folk made necessary.

In this development - which Heydrich indivisibly bound to the SS, although it elevated him above narrow considerations, and which enabled him to master the police means of the Reich's great will to create order in Europe - the Führer assigned him the Deputy Protectorship for Bohemia and Moravia. He now took over, visible to all, the function that demanded a formative energy beyond simply defensive activity. From close knowledge of inadequacy in every form and in all areas, he always formulated the concept for the best solution, regardless whether it deal with economic questions or those of cultural life. It was a big surprise for the great working mass in one of the old core regions of the Reich that the conscious seducers and saboteurs of Europe's new formation in the region of Bohemia-Moravia were indeed swiftly and ruthlessly eliminated wherever they were met, but that the firm hand proceeded generously and justly with the constructive work, where even the smallest remanent of good will could unfold in an atmosphere of trust. This free and open manner of business that was more than political skill could have produced corresponded to his personal manner.

It only completes the tragedy of his death that the bullet struck him neither in the background work as Chief of the Security Police and SD nor in combat at the war front, rather at the start of a peaceful and constructive work as Deputy Reich Protector that would benefit the Czechs, whose prosperity is undeniably tied to the Reich, not less than the German folk.

The historical mis-development to sovereignty and the time of the republic itself have educated the populace of Bohemia and Moravia away from the organic, geopolitical and historically evolved union with the Reich. The political and spiritual wirepullers of the west, the plutocratic powers and – under the cloak of a so-called pan-Slavism – the Bolshevik powers have promoted this mis-education with all means and forced the education of a recently developed, proportionally far too numerous, egotistical and ambitious intelligentsia stratum. While throughout the world, and especially in Europe, the struggle for the basic elements of a worldview raged, and while the Reich already stood in the decisive struggle to cast off the same forces, the previously mentioned development turned the region of Bohemia and Moravia into one of the most dangerous bastions against the Reich in Europe. The Führer - who, foreseeing the development of events with his prophetic insight, aimed to mobilize all forces for the decisive struggle -, therefore had to in Europe's interest oppose the forces and states that out of mis-perception of their own history endangered Europe's liberation and their own freedom.

While these forces in Bohemia and Moravia on the one hand engaged in an unprecedented armament of material kind and a spiritual agitation of the populace in the context of leadership responsibility, they were at the same time too cowardly to accept the military consequences from their previous behaviour: namely, to fight in autumn 1938. While State President Dr. Hácha, in wise recognition of the historic events returned - in terms of international law and personally - to the Reich, the government he had summoned - aside from some personnel changes hence the last government – did not accept the consequences that, based on this outward act, had to been drawn inwardly as well. Therefore, a not insignificant resistance movement could form under the eyes of that government that was able to disappoint the Reich and endanger Bohemia and Moravia in their entirety. Despite otherwise splendid intelligence about the area's affairs, it did not combat this development, either due to inability or negligence or – as some prominent examples show – consciously.

So it was left to me after being made Deputy Reich Protector to inform the State President and to make up with a firm hand what the Czech government had neglected in two and a half years. You gentlemen have a great, although also difficult, task in front of you. Your government proclamation shows that you recognized the problem in its full depth and that you are willing to do a thorough job. This work will take place on two levels. On the one hand, you will work in close contact with me and the State Secretary, forming the leadership and work circle based on mutual trust, for the solution of all tasks in this region. On the other hand you will have the difficult task to fundamentally transform the criminal development within the education and leadership of the Czech population and, certainly often opposed by misunderstanding and rejection, lead the Czech populace to their best. The main emphasis will lay in a correct and clear education of the youth.

The time of parliamentarian Ministerial resolutions that prevent a practical, active government and leadership work is finally at an end. The task of the chairman will be above all other things to always keep the unity and effectiveness of the new government in terms of the important activity for enlightenment and education consistently strong. The smaller the Ministries are in the leadership apparatus, the more active, the more successful their work can be. The prerequisites of mutual trust are that all kinds of tactics within this narrow circle of trust remain absent; one only uses tactics against opponents.

Declaration of the Deputy Reich Protector SS-Obergruppenführer Heydrich to the newly installed Protectorate government.

Speech of the Reichsführer-SS at the State Ceremony for SS-Obergruppenführer Heydrich in the Mosaic Hall of the New Reich Chancellory on June 9, 1942

With the death of SS-Obergruppenführer Reinhard Heydrich, Deputy Reich Protector in Bohemia and Moravia and Chief of the SD and the Security Police, the National Socialist movement has made another blood sacrifice to our folk's fight for freedom.

As incomprehensible to us the idea is that this radiant, great man, having barely reached the age of 38, is no longer among us and no longer fights in the middle of his friends, as irreplaceable his unique ability, combined with a character of rare purity and a reason with such penetrating logic and clarity, we would not act true to him, if we did not here before his coffin again make our own the heroic ideas of death and becoming that once moved our folk upon the death of their dearest ones.

In this spirit we want to carry out this ceremony in his honor, relating his life, telling his deeds, then return the mortal shell to the eternal cycle of all existence on this earth, and then to fight on like he had lived and fought in order to try to fill his place.

Reinhard Heydrich was born on March 7, 1904 in Halle on the Saale. He attended elementary school and reformed gymnasium. Already in his school years, which after 1918 fell in the period of our folk's great decline, the young student, 16 years old, with his burning love for Germany, volunteered as a courier in the Freikorps "Märker" and was active as a volunteer in the Freikorps "Halle" in then so red central Germany. In the year 1922, in an era that rejected everything soldierly, he joined the navy as an enthusiastic officer cadet. In 1926 he became Lieutenant and in 1928 a Lieutenant Senior Grade at Sea. As radio and communications officer he was active in the most diverse branches and expanded his view through foreign travel.

In the year 1931 he left the navy. Through one of his friends, then SS-Obergruppenführer von Eberstein, I learned about him and brought him into the Schutzstaffel in July of that year. Heydrich, previously a Senor Lieutenant, joined the small Hamburg SS unit as a SS-private, where - along with the good and mostly unemployed youths who were the first start there - he did his duty in meeting hall battles and propaganda in the numerous red sections of the city. Soon afterward I brought him to me in Munich and gave him his new duties in the still quite small Reich leadership of the SS.

With his born loyalty and tenacity, he stood his ground in the politically so difficult autumn days of 1932 that placed so many demands.

When I became Police President in Munich on March 12, 1933, I immediately assigned him the so-called political department of the presidium. In the shortest time this department was reorganized and in a few weeks the Bavarian Political Police emerged from it. Soon the Political Police in every German province aside from Prussia were formed according to its pattern, until on April 20, 1934 the Prussian Minister President, our Reich Marshal Party Comrade Hermann Göring, turned over leadership of Prussia's Secret State Police to me and my deputy, SS-Brigadeführer Reinhard Heydrich. In 1936 Heydrich, 32 years old, became Chief of the Security Police within the Reich Police newly established by the Führer. Aside from the Secret State Police the whole criminal police was hence under his command.

The years 1933, 34, 35 and 36 were filled with much work and countless startup difficulties, with energetic, carefree action abroad against emigrants and traitors, with hard, painful fulfillment of duty domestically and with the most difficult task, to gain respect, esteem and rights for the new police, especially for Heydrich's Security Service, within the administrative and organizational apparatus of the provinces and of the Reich.

At the start of 1938 the Security Police was in every way an apparatus already largely firm and equipped for all tasks. It can be safely said today that the bloodless march into Austria, Sudetenland and Bohemia-Moravia as well as the liberation of Slovakia was largely owed to Heydrich through his careful identification and conscientious evaluation of all opponents and a usually very detailed, clear insight into the activity of the enemies in these countries, their organizations and their ringleaders.

I wish to set forth in public the ideas of this man feared by subhumans, hated and defamed by Jews and other criminals, and once misunderstood even by many Germans.

All the measures and actions he took, he did as a National Socialist and SS man. From the depth of his heart and his blood he fulfilled, understood and accomplished Adolf Hitler's worldview. All the problems he had to solve, he approached with the fundamental recognition of genuine, racial worldview and with the knowledge that purity, security and protection of our blood is the highest law. He had the difficult task to build and lead an organization that dealt almost exclusively with life's dark side, with inadequacies, deviations and with misunderstanding as well as with evil intent, with criminal drives and asocial elements of human society. The greatest burden on the nation's Security Service and its men is that happy events are hardly presented to them.

Heydrich rightfully took the standpoint that only the best of our folk, racially most carefully selected, endowed with exemplary character and pure spirit, with a good heart and a boundless, strong will, were suited to perform this useful service in a positive way for the whole by combatting the negative, and to bear the severity of this responsibility.

He had an unimpeachable sense of justice. Flatterers and pretenders only triggered his deep and open contempt. True and decent men could, even if they were guilty, always hope for his chivalrous attitude and human understanding. But he never let anything happen, despite all understanding for the often so tragic problem of the individual, that would have harmed the whole nation or the future of our blood. As in all things, he approached the question of criminality with healthy common sense. But at the same time he made sure that the German criminal police received the most modern technical and scientific equipment. As head of the International Criminal Police Commission he made valuable contributions as a comrade to the police throughout the world with his knowledge and his experiences. It was above all his accomplishment that from the year 1936 onward criminality in Germany steadily declined and despite the war, now in its third year, reached the lowest level ever. May all people in Germany who, even during blackouts – in contrast to the "glorious, humane" democratic countries – can walk the streets calmly, unmolested and without being robbed, be thankful in their hearts to Reinhard Heydrich. Whether common or political criminals are concerned, who are both the opponents of the nation, they were again and again seized by an iron hand, and they will in the future, too, be caught by his men of the Security Police.

From countless conversations with Heydrich I also know how this man, who had to be outwardly so hard and strict, often suffered and struggled, and what it many times cost him to nonetheless again and again decide and act according to the law of the SS, that obligates us to "spare neither our own nor foreign blood, if the life of the nation demands it". In this sense did he, one of the best educators in National Socialist Germany, train the SS leadership corps of the Reich Security Police, leading and making it great with unconditional purity.

The SS leaders and men under his command were devoted with heartfelt love and respect for their commander who always stepped in them for, who even in the most difficult cases stood by his men and covered them, a gentleman by birth and bearing. He was an equally shining example in the readiness to bear responsibility as he was an example of modesty. He took the standpoint that it was better to let the work done speak for itself than to push oneself to the forefront. Many of those he allowed to glimpse inside the Reich Security Service's intellectual work in spheres of life were surprised. No trace was to be found of the old musty, jailer criminal police. The basics were processed with strictest scientific research and only then on their basis daily issues approached.

Then the war came with all its many tasks in the newly occupied territories, in Poland, in Norway, in the Netherlands, in Belgium, France, Yugoslavia and Greece, but above all in Russia.

It was hard for him, this energetic fighter and go-getter, not to be allowed to go to the foremost front. Next to his never-tiring work, which he performed day and night as one of the most industrious men in the Reich, he took time in the morning for weeks and months to gradually earn his pilot's license and pass his examine as a fighter pilot. In 1940 he flew over Holland and Norway as a fighter pilot and acquired there the Bronze Front Flight Bar and the Iron Cross Second Class. But he was not satisfied with that.

In 1941, at the start of the Russian campaign, he flew again without my knowledge – and I can attest with proud joy that this was the only secret he kept from me in the eleven years of our shared path – as a fighter pilot with a German squadron in Southern Russia and there acquired the Silver Front Flight Bar and the Iron Cross First Class.

In that period fate had already stretched out its hand for him. He had been shot down by Russian flak, but fortunately landed between the lines and fought his way through to the German side, in order to immediately go up again the next morning in another plane.

As much as I had always taken the standpoint that Heydrich was more important at his post than in military service at the front, I nonetheless completely understood his drive. He wanted to also fulfill and prove the part of the law "not to spare our own blood" at the front, although his whole activity as Chief of the SD was a daily, dangerous service.

September of last year brought him a new, great – and as we today know – the final, great task. The Führer made him Deputy Reich Protector in the Protectorate Bohemia-Moravia after Reich Protector von Neurath fell ill. Many in Germany, and above all in th Czech folk, believed back then that if this feared Heydrich came, he would govern only through blood and terror.

But in these months, when he was for the first time given a visible, positive, creative task the whole world could see, his ingenious talents showed themselves to a vast extent. He interceded harshly, grabbed the guilty, gained unconditional respect for German power and the Reich's might, but gave to all those of good will the chance to cooperate. There was no problem in the diverse life in these Reich lands of Bohemia and Moravia that this young Deputy Reich Protector did not handle and - with the strength of his heart, the deep understanding of the laws of our blood and his permeation with the Reich myth – successfully put on the path toward solution, and in part already solve.

But on May 27 the insidious bomb of British origin, thrown by a paid subject from the ranks of lowest sub-humanity, brought him down. Fear and excessive carefulness were alien to him, one of the best athletes in the SS, a daring fencer, rider, swimmer, marathoner – a sportsman in ability and in attitude.

Characteristic for his courage and his energy is that, although seriously wounded himself, he still defended himself and fired twice at the assassin.

For days we hoped that his healthy body – thanks to the strength of his healthy ancestors and his own simple and disciplined life – would overcome the grave danger. On the seventh day, June 4, 1942, fate, God, the ancient one – in whom he, the great opponent of the misuse of any religion for political purposes, deeply believed with self-evident unerring and subordination – completed corporeal life.

Of all us, especially the leaders of the Reich he served with the full loyalty of his heart, and we, his friends and comrades– and both of his little sons, who are here as witnesses to the infinitely happy family life and as representatives of their brave mother who is expecting another child – are assembled to pay him our final respects.

The Führer awarded him the Wounded Badge in Gold and honored him on the day of his death by giving a Waffen-SS regiment on the eastern front, the 6th SS-Infantry-Standard, the name "Reinhard Heydrich".

He will live on in our holy conviction that was his faith as well. But just as he has continued the line of his ancestors and gave them only honor, so will he live on - with all his traits as a musical person and as a brave fighter, as a happy and serious, never bending spirit, a character of pure stamp, noble, decent and clean - in his sons, in the children who are heirs of his blood and name.

Our whole affection and loving care are due his wife and these children. They should be kept safe in the great family of the Schutzstaffel.

Beyond that, he will live on in our order-community of the SS. The memory of him will help us, when we must solve tasks for the Führer and the Reich:

He will struggle and fight with is, when we, true to the law, assemble, attack and hold on as the last.

He will be with us so, when we in good times and in bad eternally remain the same.

He will also be with us, however, when sit we together among comrades and celebrate.

For the Security Service and the Security Police he will, as creator and founder, also hover before the eyes of each individual as an example that will perhaps never be equaled.

For all Germans, however, as a martyr he will be an admonisher that Bohemia and Moravia are and will remain Reich lands as they have been long since.

Over there, in the other world, along with our old comrades Weitzel, Moder, Herrmann, Mülverstedt, Stahlecker and many others, he will live in the long battalions of dead SS-men and in spirit eternally fight in our ranks.

It is our holy obligation to avenge his death, to take up his task and now, without mercy and weakness now, to destroy the enemies of our folk.

I myself have just one more thing to say:

You, Reinhard Heydrich, have truly been a good SS-man!

Personally, I thank you for here for your unchanging loyalty and for the wonderful friendship that bound us in this life and that death can not separate!

The Führer

I have but few words to devote to this dead man.

He was one of the best National Socialists, one of the strongest defenders of the German Reich idea, one of the greatest opponents of all enemies of this Reich. He has fallen as a blood martyr for the preservation and protection of the Reich.

As leader of the party and as leader of the German Reich I give you, my dear comrade Heydrich, after party comrade Todt as the second German, the highest decoration that I have to award: The Highest Level of the German Order.

IV.
The Life of
Reinhard Heydrich

Childhood and Youth

Reinhard Tristan Eugene Heydrich was born on March 7, 1904 in Halle on the Saale. He was the son of Richard Bruno Heydrich and Elisabeth Marie Anna Amalie Krantz. The father was a composer and at the time of Reinhard's birth the director of the Halle school of music that he had founded. Bruno Heydrich was an admirer of the musical words of Richard Wagner. Reinhard was named after the heroes of the fourth opera of his father's "Amen". The family had two other children: Maria (1901) and Heinz Siegfried (1905). Long before he went to school, he learned to read music. At five he started to play the violin. After elementary school, where he was considered a gifted and industrious pupil, he attended the Reform Gymnasium on the Hedwigstrasse in Halle on the Saale. Here he learned modern languages like English and French, Latin, German and history as well as the natural sciences like chemistry, physics and mathematics. Former classmates later remembered that Reinhard Heydrich's grades were very good. For example, he wrote German essays reminiscent of philosophical treatises. After Germany lost the war in 1918 due to treason and the humiliating conditions of the Treaty of Versailles were felt everywhere, the Heydrich family experienced great economic need, too. During the civil war Reinhard Heydrich was a Freikorps soldier: from 1919 to 1920 he served in the Freikorps Märker and in the Freikorps Halle. Furthermore, he belonged to the Deutschvölksichen Schutz- und Trutzbund from 1920 to 1922.

Enlistment in the Navy

Reinhard Heydrich's decision to become a naval officer was a result of the following circumstances. During summer vacations, which he and his family spent in Schwinemünde, he had seen the navy and was very impressed by the order, precision and discipline. The influence of the famous Admiral Felix Graf von Luckner also played a big role. Graf Luckner was often a guest in the Heydrich home and his book "The Sea Devil" was one of Reinhard's favorites. After he passed his Abitur exam, he enlisted in the navy on March 39, 1922 in Kiel-Holtenau. In his luggage was the violin his father had given him as a going away present. Reinhard Heydrich began service as a sea cadet with crew 22. The basic training in Kiel was very difficult for him. He differed from his comrades through his musical talent. Furthermore, the navy during the Weimar period tried to look "democratic", and it did not meet his expectations. After completion of basic training came six months on broad training on the line ship "Braunschweig". From April to June 1923 he was a cadet on the sailing school ship "Niobe". From July 1, 1923 to the end of March 1934 he served on the cruiser "Berlin". Here he met for the first time then Corvette-Captain and later Chief of German Counterintelligence Wilhelm Canaris, the traitor. He, too, had been sent to the cruiser as first office on July 1, 1923. The men became friends and Heydrich was often a guest in Cararis' home, where he usually played music with his friend's wife, Erika – usually compositions by Mozart and Hayden.

On April 1, 1924 he became am ensign and went with his crew to the naval school at Mürwick, where he remained until March 1925. Reinhard was by this time already an enthusiastic athlete, successful as fencer, marksman, sailor, swimmer and rider. After he had already become Ensign Senior Class, he was promoted on October 1, 1926 – while serving on the line ship "Schleswig-Holstein" – to Lieutenant at Sea. According to his wish he was trained as a communications officer. He also perfected his command of foreign languages like Russian, Spanish, French and English. Promotion to Senior Lieutenant at Sea followed on July 1, 1928. He now gained a position of confidence as auxilliary lecturer and communications officer in the Admiral Staff Directorship at the naval station on the Baltic Sea. His superiors evaluated him positively. Heydrich's teacher at the naval communications school, later Vice-Admiral Gustav Kleikamp, believed his talents, knowledge and ability were above average.

During those years Reinhard Heydrich studied a lot of political literature. Reading "Mein Kampf" contributed to his view of Adolf Hitler as the man who could liberate Germany from being led around by the nose by international regulations.

On December 30, 1930 he met 18 year old Lina von Osten at a ball of the Sleswig-Holstein Sailing and Rowing Club in Kiel. She came from Avendorf on the Baltic Sea island Fehmarn, where her father was the schoolmaster. Just four days after they met Heydrich proposed marriage to her in the Wicks Vine Cellar. After a visit to the home of his future bride's parents the pair was officially engaged on Christmas Day 1930; he came with a violin case under his arm. Heydrich also sent an engagement announcement to a former pupil of the Colonial Woman's School in Rendsburg. He had met this young lady at a sailing regatta and she had later visited him in Kiel. Because no room was available, Heydrich invited her to stay with his hosts. Although there could be no talk of an "approach", the girl nonetheless thought she could reckon with a marriage proposal soon. When this expectation did not materialize, the girl's father, an influential senior member of the Naval Board of Works, demanded Heydrich to marry his daughter. When he refused, the man complained to Admiral Raeder. The result was that Heydrich had to face a naval court of honor. On the basis of that honor court's report, Admiral Raeder decided that Senior Lieutenant Reinhard Heydrich should be discharged from the navy. His world collapsed. Together with his fiance he travelled back to his parents in Halle. It is interesting to note that so far not one single document regarding this honor court case has been found in the archives. Heydrich himself repeatedly said he was convinced that he had been removed from the navy for political reasons.

A New Path

In this time of great unemployment Heydrich stood before nothingness. He had to find a position. An opportunity presented itself to become a teacher at the Hanseatic Yacht School in Neustadt with a salary of 380 marks. But that kind of position did not suit him; he only wanted to be a soldier. Heydrich's mother asked Frau von Eberstein, who was the aunt of Reinhard's godmother, for advice. Her son, Freiherr Karl von Eberstein, was at that time SA-Oberführer and leader of the SA in Münich/Upper Bavaria. He had good connections with the SA Chief of Staff Ernst Röhm as well as with the Reichsführer-SS Heinrich Himmler. Elisabeth Heydrich inquired whether Karl von Ebrstein could provide her son with a good position in the NSDAP. Heydrich was not interested in a position in the SA, because he considered that organization too small compensation for the loss of his career as sea officer. His fiance recommended to him to join the Schutzstaffel (SS) of the NSDAP. This small, absolutely military organization was the elite of National Socialism.

On June 1, 1931 Reinhard Heydrich became a member of the NSDAP (party number 544916). Von Eberstein arranged a meeting with Heinrich Himmler in the latter's private residence in Waldtrudering, a Munich suburb. Himmler was just looking for a capable man to build an intelligence service of the SS. He gave Heydrich twenty minutes to put down on paper how he viewed such a task. Heydrich wrote down his ideas, designed a suitable organizational model and presented the results to the Reichsführer. He was very impressed and immediately decided to employ Heydrich. On July 14, 1931 he joined the Hamburg SS. He was now an SS man with the SS number 10,120. His monthly salary was set at 180 marks.

On December 26, 1931, the marriage of Reinhard Heydrich and Lina von Osten took place in the village church of Grossenrode. SA and SS men formed a lane wearing white shirts and black pants because of the uniform ban; the organist played the Horst Wessel Song when they left the church. At that time Heydrich was already an SS-Sturmbannführer.

On August 10, 1931 Heydrich had started his service as head of department I-c. His first office was a room in the Brown House that he had to share with Richard Hildebrandt, Sepp Dietrich's Chief of Staff of the SS Group South. Back then Heydrich did not even have his own typewriter, so Hildebrandt loaned him his for hours. An efficiently organized enemy index emerged from the files Himmler had turned over to him. At the end of 1931 two rooms were rented for the SS-Ic in the fifth stock of Munich's Türkenstrase 23. That was the residence of party comrade and widow Viktoria Edrich. She was an especially reliable and loyal National Socialist. The blood flag that was carried at the head of the November 9, 1923 Putsch was stored in her clothes closet during the time the SA and SS were banned.

At the start of 1932 Heydrich and his wife took residence in House Number 55 in Munich's suburb of Lochhausen. Each day he took the train to the office in the Türkenstrasse. The name of the service was by now "Sicherheitsdienst" - "security service" - (SD). All SD co-workers were personally accountable to Heydrich alone. The SD, although part of the SS, was supposed to operate independently. In September 1932 the SD – as well as the Heydrichs – moved to a villa in Munich's Zuccalistrasse 4. The house was at the outlet of a dead end road. Heydrich was called "C" as head of the Security Service; his office was called "Central Office of the SD".

On June 6, 1932 Rudolf Jordan, Gauleiter (province chief) of Halle-Merseburg, sent a letter to Gregor Strasse, then Reich Organizational Leader of the NSDAP, in which he mentioned the rumor that Reinhard Heydrich's father was a Jew. The genealogist Dr. Achim Gercke was assigned to investigate the matter. On June 22, 1932 he reported that "former naval lieutenant Reinhardt (sic) Heydrich is of German descent and free of colored or Jewish blood." In his letter Dr. Gercke explained the origin of the rumor that led to the vernacular of Heydrich's father being called "Isidor Süss" and finally to the suspicion that the family was of Jewish origin. He wrote: "The genealogy shows that Senior Lieutenant Heydrich's grandmother Ernestine Wilhelmine Heydrich, maiden name Lindner, was married a second time with the locksmith assistant Gustav Robert Süss; as the mother of several children from the marriage with her first husband, Reinhold Heydrich, she often called herself 'Süss-Heydrich'. Furthermore, it is noteworthy that the assistant Süss as well was not of Jewish origin." Despite Dr. Gercke's assessment, there are still many rumors about Reinhard Heydrich's so-called Jewish background.

On January 30, 1933 Adolf Hitler was named Reich Chancellor by Reich President von Hindenburg. Three days before the rise to power SS-Standartenführer Heyrich left his position as chief of staff of the security service and was assigned to the staff of the Reichsführer-SS as SS-Standartenführer for special tasks. He was hence made equal to the Office Chief in the Staff of the Reichsführer-SS.

The Bavarian government resisted the National Socialist rise to power. For that reason, General Franz Ritter von Epp was supposed to be named Reich Governor of Bavaria. But that was rejected by the Bavarian Ministerial Council. General von Epp's appointment document was ready in Berlin, which was later telegraphed to the Bavarian provincial government in Munich. Reinhard Heydrich knew, too, that it was very important for the officials in Bavaria to indeed receive that telegram. He marched with an assault troop of SS-men to the Munich telegraph office and - pistol in hand – took the telegram from Berlin. That very same night Ritter von Epp formed the National Socialist provincial government. Reichsführer-SS Heinrich Himmler was named Police President of the Police Directory of Munich. Reinhard Heydrich became head of the Political Department (Dept. VI) in the Presidium. A few weeks later Himmler became Bavaria's Political Police Commander and Heydrich head of the newly founded Bavarian Political Police (BPP).

As Chief of the Security Service of the Reichsführer-SS he decided to move his office to Berlin. Suitable quarters were found on the Branitzer Platz at the Eichenallee corner. In Munich the SD established a new residence in the Leopoldstrasse. Heydrich rented a private residence at Ainmillerstrasse 10. On June 17, 1933 the Heydrich couple's first son was born, Klaus. Promotion to SS-Brigadeführer followed on November 9, 1933. Reinhard Heydrich was one of the first men to receive the SS Death's Head ring on December 24, 1933. The SD has meanwhile become its own SS office with headquarters in the Wittelsbacher palace in Munich in the Briennerstrasse. It should also be mentioned that Reinhard Heydrich and his SD played an important role in crushing the Röhm revolt. The SA Chief of Staff, Ernst Röhm - who tried to end Adolf Hitler's leadership of the NSDAP and direct the party himself - was shot along with several helpers after proof of his treasonous activity was produced. Through his behaviour he had put the Reich and all of the constructive work of National Socialism in great danger. For his services Heydrich was promoted to SS-Gruppenführer, effective June 30, 1934. Adolf Hitler's decree of July 20, 1934 elevated the SS to an independent organization within the NSDAP; it was no longer subordinate to the SA.

In November and December 1934 the SD moved from Bavaria to the Reich capital. New quarters were established in the Prince Albert Palace on Berlin's Wilhelmstrasse 102. On December 28, 1934 a second son was born, Heider.

At the end of 1934 Heydrich decided to build a summer house on some property in Burg on the island of Fehmarn. The architect Gustav Rall was supposed to design it. In May 1935 the workmen started construction. When it was finished the Reichsführer-SS was the sponsor at the completion ceremony. On March 6, 1935 the first issue of the weekly newspaper "Das Schwarze Korps" appeared.

Although the Reichsführer-SS had appointed 25 year old Gunter d'Alquen the chief editor, Heydrich was certainly the driving force behind this newspaper, whose readers even included the Führer. He wrote many articles in the "Schwarze Korps". The best known one is his publication "The Changes in our Struggle" published in 1935 by the Franz Eher Verlag, Munich-Berlin.

On June 17, 1936 a decree by the Führer and Reich Chancellor created the new Reich police. Reinhard Heydrich, 32 years old, because the Chief of the Security Police. In addition to the Secret State Police the whole of the criminal police was subordinate to him. The years until the breakout of the war were filled with much work and many startup difficulties. Many actions against enemies inside and outside the Reich were carried out. On September 27, 1939 the Reich Security Main Office (RSHA) emerged with the following departments:

Department I: Personnel Issues
Department II: Organization, Administration and Law
Department III: German Living Areas
Department IV: Gestapo
Department V: Reich Criminal Police
Department VI: Foreign Intelligence
Department VII: Archives

At the end of February 1937 Heydrich and his family moved into a new residence at Auguststrasse 14 in Berlin-Schlachtensee. On April 9, 1939 the family's third child was born, their daughter Silke.

Accomplishments in Greater Germany's Fight for Freedom

Since the Führer's generous peace proposals were ignored by Poland and England while Polish atrocities against ethnic Germans escalated alarmingly, the Führer declared the start of military action against the Polish aggressors on September 1, 1939.

Now that the war had begun, Heydrich decided to prove himself as a soldier at the front as well. He initially just asked Luftwaffe General Lörtzer for permission to fly along. His first combat flight was as a dome gunner in a formation of Destroyer Squadron 55 on September 12, 1939. At the military airport Staaken near Berlin he trained in the early morning hours before going to work in order to eventually get a pilot's license and pass his test as fighter pilot. He became pilot of a ME 109 decorated with his crest and family coat-of-arms. During the Norwegian campaign he flew many reconnaissance missions from Stavanger over England and Scotland. For his heroic action he was decorated with the Bronze Front Pilot Bar and the Iron Cross Second Class. In mid-May he returned to Berlin. On August 28, 1940 he took over leadership of the International Criminal Police Commission and on December 16, 1940 he was named by the Reich Sport Leader, effective January 1, 1941, Reich Professional Fencer in the NS Reich Federation for Physical Exercise. At the start of the Russian campaign he flew again as fighter pilot with a German squadron in southern Russia. He was shot down once by the Russians along the Beresina. Landing behind enemy lines, he hid for two days and two nights while he walked back to the German lines. The Luftwaffe rewarded him with the Silver Front Pilot Bar and the Iron Cross First Class.

The Jewish Question

"The Jew has always been the mortal enemy of all Nordic-led and racially healthy folks. His goal was and remains domination of the world by a more or less visible Jewish elite. Every folk that has, in times of political and weakness, allowed the immigration and above all later the racial mixture with the Jews, has been systematically decayed." Reinhard Heydrich wrote these words in 1935 in his publication "The Changes in our Struggle".

Contrary to what postwar writers claim, the goal of National Socialist Germany was not the physical extermination of the Jewish folk, rather combating the Jewish influence felt by all strata within the folk community to be oppressive. Already in the 1930s, German government offices had launched initiatives in order to - in cooperation with Jewish organizations - promote the emigration of Jewish citizens. The first Jewish expert of the SD and Chief of Department II 112, Leopold Edler von Mildenstein, was the proponent of this policy. Born in Prague, he had achieved a reputation as an expert on the Middle East while working as a degreed engineer and coworker of the *Berlin Börsenzeitung*; by travelling much abroad and through personal connections he had established many contacts with Zionist organizations. In 1934 he travelled to Palestine and later published a travel report with the title "A Nazi travels to Palestine".

Emigration was regulated by the government above all by two agreements: the "Haavara" and the "Rublee-Wohlttat-Agreement".

The word "Haavara" is Hebrew and means "the transfer" or "the transport". In this case it meant the transfer of wealth and property. The Haavara included the regulation: Jews who want to emigrate to Palestine can deposit their wealth into one or several accounts at two specific Jewish banks in Germany. They can even deposit it if they wish to remain in Germany for the time being. They could freely use this money for the benefit of Jewish settlers already in Palestine. They could also invest the money in Palestine.

The basic idea of the "Rublee-Wohlthat-Agreement" was this: an internationally overseen trust fund should be established to which 25% of the Jewish wealth inside Germany should be transferred. Foreign creditors should for their part also contribute to the emigration, which the Reich government would repay at a 20 year rate in foreign currency. Each emigrant was to receive in addition to the necessary travelling money minimum capital to establish his existence. Initially, 150,000 Jews capable of work were to emigrate, later followed by their family members.

The court historians always connect Heydrich's name with the "holocaust" by claiming that he was chairman at the so-called Wannsee conference on January 20, 1942. But it is questionable whether such a conference really took place. Examination of the "Wannsee Protocols" shows that they are a fake. Lacking are the name of the issuing office, its file number, the notarization (that it is indeed a genuine copy of the original) and the date. Also lacking are the distributor or at least identification for whom this copy was meant as well as the receipt stamp of the receiving office. The lacking of such information is inconceivable for an official German government document, especially such an important one. Merely the file number of the recipient is given. It is also noteworthy that it was typed on a typewriter lacking the SS symbol. Hence this copy could not have been produced by a higher SS office. The paper format is also unusual.

Furthermore, it is not possible that Reinhard Heydrich chaired the so-called Wannsee conference, because on that day he was in Prague for the installment of the new Protectorate Government. Upon consideration of the circumstances, especially the winter weather and Heydrich's own schedule, the question arises why he would have made two appointments so far apart on the day, and indeed without any apparent necessity.

It should also be clearly stated here that there were no execution gas chambers in German concentration camps. Zyklon B (cyanide) was indeed used at Auschwitz, but only to delouse the clothing of new prisoners. The danger of pestilence is always high at such dense concentrations of people in confined space and with such poor hygienic conditions as are unavoidable in camps. This threat can only be combatted by the strictest hygienic measures, which is why the SS paid such close attention to this task in all concentration camps. In this connection one should remember that World Jewry had already on March 24, 1935 declared war on Germany. The Jews used their influence on the media and the world economy and waged a global boycott against Germany. German concentration camps were not extermination camps, rather internment camps for members of a hostile nation.

Deputy Reich Protector in Bohemia and Moravia

On March 15, 1939 the Protectorate Bohemia-Moravia was founded. Reich Minister Freiherr Constantin von Neurath was named Reich Protector by Adolf Hitler. Karl Hermann Frank from Karlsbad became State Secretary as well as leader of the SS-Region Bohemia-Moravia. Reichsführer-SS Heinrich Himmler also made him the higher SS and police leader in the protectorate. In September 1941 a dangerous situation had arisen in Bohemia and Moravia. The Czecho-slovakian exile government in London agitated the protectorate's populace to resist the German authorities. After the start of the campaign against the Soviet Union the illegal activity of the communist underground also increased. The protectorate was of great importance to the German armaments industry. For example, the Skoda-Works in Pilsen were vital to the war effort. Any reduction of armaments production would have great consequences for the German soldiers fighting against Bolshevism. It was clear that the leadership of the Greater German Reich had to take measures in order to counter this development. Reinhard Heydrich had received reports from the Commander of the Security Police and SD in Prague, Dr. Horst Böhme, about the bed of unrest in the country. It was soon shown that these reports were correct. The number of pure sabotage acts swelled and reached an unprecedented extent. Especially frequent were cut telephone lines, train car arson and cut brake lines. Machines in armament factories were intentionally damaged as demanded by resistance slogans. Resistance arsonists set fire to supply warehouses and factory buildings. In August 1941 gas storage tanks with 100,000 liters of fuel went up in flames.

In the week of September 14-21, 1941 the Czech protectorate press was boycotted in accordance with instructions from London radio. The boycott was pursued so extensively that over half the edition went back to the respective publishers. Resistance stiffened more and more. The high point came on September 20, 1941 in Lettowitz near Brunn with a bomb attack against an institution where 84 German children lived as part of the wartime program to relocate German children to the relatively safe countryside.

The SD reports were sent through Heydrich's office to the Führer and Reichsleiter Martin Bormann as well. On September 22, 1942 a conference about the necessary measures was to be held in the Führer headquarters Wolfschanze near Rastenburg.

The first invited conference guest, State Secretary Frank, arrived in the Führer headquarters already on the morning of September 21, 1941. He was received by the Führer and made a presentation about the political situation in Bohemia and Moravia. That same name Heydrich was also called to the Führer headquarters, where he arrived in the late afternoon. Together with the Reichsführer-SS Himmler and Frank he presented the origins and the organization of the Czech resistance to the Führer. Adolf Hitler was very impressed by Reinhard Heydrich's vast professional knowledge. The conferences were continued the next day. The result was that on September 27, 1941 the Führer assigned Heydrich to take over the business of the Reich Protector in Bohemia and Moravia. Three days earlier, on September 24, 1941, he had already been promoted to SS-Obergruppenführer and General of the Police. He retained the office of Chief of the Reich Security Main Office. In order to be able to perform his duties in Prague and Berlin, two airplanes were placed at his disposal; when it was not possible to fly, he travelled by train. The same evening he arrived, he declared a state of civil emergency, whereby all anti-Reich acts and sabotage fell under martial law. The decree announced was on the radio on September 27, 1941 at 22:00 and publicized the next day in the press and through posters. From the time Heydrich took office until the state of emergency ended, 404 people were sentenced to death by martial courts. They were political conspirators, black-marketeers, racketeers, saboteurs and Jews. Heydrich had proof that Czech Minister-President General Alois Elias was in contact with the resistance movement and with the exile-government in London. He was arrested and sentenced to death by the people's court in Prague.

Despite the severity of the measures Heydrich was able to call up positive, agreeable voices within the Czech populace. During a symbolic ceremony on the Wenzels chapel of the Prague Castle on November 19, 1941, Heydrich received into the Reich's protection the jewels of Bohemian coronation. State President Dr. Hácha presented him with the seven keys to the coronation chamber. Heydrich returned three of these seven keys to the custody of the State President with the words, "View this equally as trust and obligation". With Heydrich's approval Dr. Hácha formed a new government. The former Justice Minister, university professor Dr, Jaroslav Krejci, became chairman of the government and was again named Justice Minister. Dr. Richard Bienert was Minister of the Interior, Dr. Josef Kalfus was Minister of Finance, Colonel Dr. Emanuel Moravec was Minister for Schooling and Folk Education as well as head of the Office for Folk Enlightenment, SS-Oberführer Dr. Walter Bertsch was Minister for Work and Economy, Dr. Heinrich Kamenicky was Minister of Transportation and Dr. Adolf Hruby was Minister for Agriculture and Forestry.

After installment of the new government Heydrich ended the state of civil emergency in order to demonstrate that one trusted the protectorate's populace. Thanks to his personal contact to Herbert Backe, State Secretary in the Ministry of Agriculture, the fat rations for two million workmen could be put on par with those in the old Reich. Beside that, Heydrich was able to put two million pairs of shoes at the disposal of the Czech work force. They were distributed free of charge in factories by plant councils and unions. Cigarettes confiscated from blackmarketeers were also given to the workers. Among the Deputy Reich Protector's measures were reform of social welfare and social security insurance. Here, too, the standards of the Czech Republic, initially in force in the Protectorate as well, had been far below those of the Greater German Reich. Heydrich passed decrees that improved social security insurance for workers and miners and increased benefits without simultaneously raising the contributions. On Heydrich's orders the Day of Labor, May 1, 1942, was moved to a Saturday, so that the workers would have two free days in a row.

At that time the six day work week was still general practice. Saturday was usually a workday. He donated 116,000 movie tickets and 18,000 theatre tickets to the workers in Prague alone. The soccer game for the mastership of the national league was moved ahead to the May holiday and the admittance tickets were distributed by an organization subordinate to the unions. To crown the whole affair, on the occasion of the May Day holiday Heydrich officially proclaimed something he had already announced as a plan at the end of October 1941: he transformed luxury hotels in Bad Luhatschowitz into worker recreation resorts. On May 1 three thousand Czech armaments workers were given a vacation; the total in 1942 was seven thousand. Selection was made by the employer in conjunction with the plant council. Heydrich received delegations of Czech peasants and workers in the Prague Castle and visited factories and large plants, where he talked with Czech workers. He totally reorganized the bureaucracy. Bypassing official channels, he paid substantial sums of money and pensions to injured members and survivors of the Czech gendarmerie who had engaged the resistance. A coachman who had significantly contributed to the investigation of a bombing in traditionally unquiet Kladno was given a premium of 10,000 kroner from Protectorate sources. The same sum was presented to the family of the gendarmerie ensign Kominek who had been seriously wounded in the bombing. The widow of Gendarmerie Lieutenant Ometak, who had been gunned down by the resistance, received the same sum as well as a pension in the amount of his last full salary. He gave wounded Czech policemen a German pistol with his personal dedication; their children received a savings account with a decent sum.

Heydrich had been greatly impressed by Prague's unique architecture. He developed architectural plans in order to transform Prague into a German city and to connect it with the Reich by means of the Autobahn.

As Deputy Reich Protector of Bohemia and Moravia Reinhard Heydrich and his family resided barely twenty kilometers northwest of Prague at the manor Jungfern-Breschau. Here his family life flourished. Although a city residence at Hradschin also stood at his disposal, he seldom spent the night there. In that period Heydrich read many history books that dealt with Bohemia and its relationship with the Reich. The figure of Albert von Wallenstein especially fascinated him. He had read everything available about Wallenstein. On Sundays he took many trips to Friedland, Wallenstein's ancestral home. All of the outworks were also visited. Over the course of time he had gained an impression of all of Wallenstein's widely dispersed lands. But his historical interest extended beyond that. For example, he went to Melnik and visited the grave of the holy Ludmilla; he was also interested in excavations at the Prague Castle that the German university of Prague carried out.

Heydrich had success with the achievement of his goals. Adolf Hitler, too, was very satisfied with what had been achieved in the protectorate. It has even been claimed that the Führer intended Reinhard Heydrich to be his successor.

Assassination and Death

Due to Reinhard Heydrich's successful, constructive work in Bohemia and Moravia the Czechoslovakian exile-government in London viewed him as the most dangerous opponent on the German side. In cooperation with the British Special Operations Executive (SOE) Eduard Benesch, who considered himself President in exile, developed plans to assassinate the Deputy Reich Protector. The code name for this plan was "Anthropoid". Two non-commissioned officers of the former Czechoslovakian army, Jan Kubis and Josef Gabcik, were assigned to carry it out. Together with a few other men they landed by parachute in the protectorate on the night of 28/29 December 1941. During the following months they hid in the underground and spent their time trying to get an impression of Heydrich's habits.

Altogether three variations of the assassination plan were developed.

The first called for a bomb attack against Heydrich's train car. That plan was rejected, because the target was too fast and unsure.

A second plan centered on the country road at Jungfern-Breschau, but this plan, too, could not be carried out because of the presence of an SS guard in front of the ground's wall consisting of a platoon of Security Police.

So the murderers decided on the third plan. There was a very sharp curve in Lieben, a district within the city of Prague. The Deputy Reich Protector's vehicle would have to go into a lower gear because of the curve and sharp decline, and at that moment Kubis and Gabcik wanted to murder Heydrich.

An increase of communist acts of sabotage, strikes and unrest as well as a resistance movement agitated and financed by London pushed the development in France and Belgium to a high-point. In order to restore calm and security in those lands, Adolf Hitler intended to assign Heydrich similar tasks in France and Belgium as in Bohemia and Moravia. After he had already prepared new occupation statutes for occupied France, he was supposed to fly to Berlin on May 27, 1942 for a conference with the Führer. With the help of a resistance informant, the assassins and their helpers knew Heydrich's departure date. On May 27 Kubis and Gabcik stood at that corner. Czech SOE agent Josef Valcik was stationed above the curve. His task was to signal the arrival of Heydrich's vehicle with a whistle or pocket mirror. The dark green Mercedes 320 driven by SS-Oberscharführer Johannes Klein approached around 10:30. He drove with the top down and license plate number SS-4. It is generally assumed it was a vehicle with the license plate number was S-3, but that is not correct. License plate SS-3 belonged to Heydrich's Mercedes 770. This misunderstanding originated in a long-distance message by the Reich Criminal Police Office that mistakenly identified the vehicle as SS-3. When the vehicle, coming from the Kirchmaier Strasse, was about to turn into the Klein-Holeschowitz-Strasse, Gabcik aimed his Sten machine-pistol at Heydrich and pulled the trigger. But the weapon did not fire, because the murderer had forgotten to disengage the safety. Heydrich, who momentarily recognized the situation, jumped up, drew his pistol and started to fire at Gabcik. The driver stopped the vehicle in order to participate in the hunt for the assassin. But this made the Mercedes and both passengers a large, stationary target. Heydrich, reacting with lightning speed, tried to jump out of the vehicle and pursue the assassin. But before he managed that, Kubis threw the Mills special grenade. The explosive device struck right next to the vehicle's rear right wheel and immediately detonated. Heydrich was seriously injured by the splinters, but he still fought. He aimed his pistol at the second assassin and emptied the whole magazine. Mortally wounded, he then collapsed over the vehicle's hood. A blond Czech woman took care of him. A passing truck was stopped and it drove Heydrich to the Bulovka hospital.

There he was examined and it was discovered than an immediate operation was necessary. A rib was smashed; splinters and horsehair from the auto upholstery had penetrated from the back, to the left and above the diaphragm, and destroyed Heydrich's spleen. The German Chief Physician, Prof. Dr. Walter Dick, and Prof. Dr. Josef Albert Hohlbaum of the Prague University Clinic, directed the difficult operation. Reichsführer-SS Heinrich Himmler sent his friend, SS-Brigadeführer Prof. Dr. Karl Gebhardt, to Prague in order to take over the medical treatment. Gebhardt was Chief Physician at the hospital in Hohenlychen. He was accompanied by Dr. Ludwig Stumpfegger and Prof. Ferdinand Sauerbruch, a famous surgeon and friend of the Heydrich family.

Meanwhile, Heydrich seemed to be recovering well from his serious injuries and the following operation. He received many several visits from his wife Lina among others. On May 31 Heinrich Himmler visited his wounded SS comrade for the last time. During this encounter Heydrich quoted a few lines from his father's fourth opera"Amen":

*"Yes, the world is just a barrel-organ,
that our Lord himself plays. Each
must dance according to the song
that is playing on the drum at the time."*

This verse was intended to reinforce his demand that the Reichsführer-SS continue without compromise the SS policy whose goal was the emigration of the Jews from Europe.

On June 3rd Dr. Gebhardt reported that the state of Heydrich's health had improved. The fever, too, receded. But after the noon meal there was a collapse. The situation deteriorated rapidly and Heydrich lost consciousness. In the early morning hours of June 4th the doctors managed to make him conscious again. After he had said goodbye to his wife Reinhard Heydrich died of blood poisoning on June 4, 1942 at 04:30.

Until the late evening of June 5th the body remained in a guarded room of the Bulovka hospital. In the night of June 5/6 the body was taken on a gun-carriage to the Prague Castle. There it was placed in the Reinhard Heydrich hall. On the morning of June 7th the dead SS-Obergruppenführer was laid in state upon a tomb of state in the honor square of the castle. Eight SS officers continuously stood honor guard. From the early morning hours until the funeral tens of thousands of Germans and Czechs walked past Reinhard Heydrich's stretcher to show their repsects. In the presence os the Reichsführer-SS, the State President and other invited guests SS-Oberst-Gruppenführer and Senior General of the Police Kurt Daluege delivered an eulogy. After the funeral's completion the coffin was carried to the gun-carriage in front of the honor gate and secured. When the order to depart was given, the mourner procession left the Prague Castle. The destination was the train station. Formations of the party and army troops formed a lane along Prague's streets. At the train station the coffin was taken from the gun-carriage and loaded into the waiting special train bound for Berlin. The next day, June 8, 1942, the special train arrived at the Anhalter train station in Berlin at 12:00. The Reichsführer-SS, Senior General Daluege, State Secretary Frak and other dignitaries waited on the rail platform. The coffin was secured to a gun-carriage and taken to the Prince Albert Palace at Wilhelmstrasse 102. In the conference hall in was placed upon a tomb of state. Six SD honor guards took position on each side of the coffin. That night the dead man's closest co-workers stood the honor watch.

On June 9, 1942 Reinhard Heydrich's mortal remains were taken from the Prince Albert Palace to the New Reich Chancellory. The coffin was placed in the mosaic hall. Eight honor guards were posted and bowels of flame stood on both sides of the tomb of state. The Führer, who was accompanied by the Reichsführer-SS, arrived around 15:00. The state orchestra played mourning music from Richard Wagner's "Götterdämmerung". The Reichsführer-SS's eulogy followed, in which he expressed Reinhard Heydrich's significance for the National Socialist movement. Himmler said of Heydrich: "All measures and actions he took, he handled as a National Socialist and SS-man. From the depths of his heart and blood he fulfilled, understood and achieved Adolf Hitler's worldview."

After the Reichsführer-SS's address the Führer laid the wreath and said: "I have only a few words to devote to this dead man. He was one of the best National Socialists, one of the strongest defenders of ther German Reich idea, one of the greatest opponents of all enemies of this Reich. He has fallen as a martyr for the preservation and security of the Reich. As Führer of the party and as Führer of the German Reich I bestow on you, my dear comrade Heydrich, after party comrade Todt as the second German and highest decoration that I have to give: the Highest Level of the German Order."

The Führer then pinned the high order on the fallen man's order-pillow. After he had turned to both of Reinhard Heydrich's sons, he read the state ceremony.

Amid the music of the mourning march from "Eroica" by Ludwig von Beethoven the coffin with the deceased SS-Obergruppenführer was carried out of the mosaic hall. In the Wilhelmstrasse it was secured on a gun-carriage harnessed to six black horses. The mourners procession formed. The Reichsführer-SS marched behind the coffin gun-carriage. He was followed by Senior General Daluege, SS-Obergruppenführer Sepp Dietrich, State Secretary Frank and other dignitaries. The gun-carriage was driven through Berlin's streets to the Invaliden cemetery, where the great soldier Reinhard Heydrich would find his final resting place. The mourners procession arrived at the cemetery around 16:30. The coffin was taken from the gun-carriage and carried to the burial site. Coffin-bearers of the Wehrmacht lowered it into the grave. SS-Obergruppenführer Sepp Dietrich spoke the words of departure. Then the SS anthem was played as well as "Ich hatt' einen Kameraden".

In addition to the highest German decoration Reinhard Heydrich received posthumously the Wounded Badge in Gold, the War Service Cross First Class with Swords and the Blood Order. His name was entered into the honor roll of the movement's martyrs. On the day of his death a Waffen-SS regiment on the Eastern front, the 6th SS-Infantry Regiment, was given the name "Reinhard Heydrich". In the night of July 22/23, 1942 Lina bore Heydrich a daughter, whom she named Märte.

"Within the context of its worldview National Socialism does not have the intention to attack the Jewish folk in any form. The recognition of Jewry as a racial community that is based on blood, not religion, leads the German government to guarantee the racial separation of this community without any restriction. The government itself finds itself in complete agreement with the great intellectual movement within Jewry, so-called Zionism."

Chief of the Reich Security Main Office SS-Obergruppenführer Reinhard Heydrich in the SS central organ, *Das Schwarze Korps*, September 26, 1935.